SHELAGH DELANEY

A Taste of Honey

With commentary and notes by
GLENDA LEEMING *and*
ELAINE ASTON

METHUEN DRAMA

Contents

Four pages of illustrations appear at the end of the commentary

Methuen Drama Student Edition

10 9 8 7 6 5 4 3

This edition first published in 1982 by Methuen London Ltd
Reissued with additional material and a new cover design 2005 and
2008; reissued with a new cover design 2009.

Methuen Drama
A & C Black Publishers Ltd
36 Soho Square
London W1D 3QY

A Taste of Honey first published in January 1959
by Methuen & Co. Ltd; new edition April 1959
A Taste of Honey copyright © 1959 by Shelagh Delaney
Commentary and notes copyright © 1982, 2005, 2008 by Methuen
Drama

ISBN 978 1 408 10601 3

Shelagh Delaney has asserted her rights under the Copyright,
Designs and Patents Act, 1988, to be identified as the author
of this play

A CIP catalogue record for this volume is available at
the British Library

Printed and bound in Great Britain by
CPI Cox & Wyman, Reading, Berkshire

*Thanks are due to Tessa Sayle and Non Worrall for their help and
advice in the preparation of this edition.*

Foreword

A Taste of Honey – Looking Back

Shelagh Delaney's *A Taste of Honey* is a play of its time and ahead of its time. Reissuing this Methuen Drama edition of the play fifty years after its first production in May 1958, by Joan Littlewood's Theatre Workshop, creates a moment to look back and to celebrate; to consider its significance and relevance to modern British theatre.

The first wave of theatre criticism concerned with 1950s British theatre saw the decade as the decade of 'anger',[1] or more specifically the decade of 'angry young men', citing John Osborne's *Look Back in Anger* (1956) as seminal to defining and characterising this angry moment, and pivotal to generating a 'New Wave' of British drama. Reassessments of the period have since invited other readings, other understandings and perspectives of '1956 and all that',[2] although Osborne and his play still cast an 'angry' (male) shadow. Hardly any women playwrights were identified as part of the New Wave. Indeed the only two to achieve any kind of prominence in what was in other ways a totally male preserve of the young, the new, or the angry were Shelagh Delaney and Ann Jellicoe (at the Royal Court).

As an isolated *female* voice in a wave of 1950s new writing, one thing Delaney did have in common with many of her male contemporaries was class. As theatre criticism at the time noted, while the new playwrights of the 1950s produced a very diverse body of work, a working-class background was something many of them shared – a factor that began to shape and authenticate their stage settings, characters, action and dialogue. In this regard Delaney was no exception. She wrote out of lived social realities, setting *A Taste of Honey* in the 'today' of her northern, industrial, home town of Salford, Lancashire. Her characters are outsiders to the relative affluence, security and social respectability of a middle-

[1] See John Russell Taylor, *Anger and After*, [1962], London: Methuen, 1969.
[2] Quotation indexes the title of Dan Rebellato's seminal reassessment of British theatre in the 1950s: *1956 and All That: The Making of Modern British Drama*, London: Routledge, 1999.

class England, and instead they articulate and authenticate the working-class character of Britain's industrial North. As Delaney took the ordinary and disadvantaged northern and working-class lives of mother (Helen) and daughter (Jo), she made them extraordinary by making them the subject of her drama; by placing them centre stage.

It was not just class and region, however, which served to figure Helen and Jo as exceptional but it was also gender. The fact that Delaney chose to make *women's* lives core to her drama was a radical move, and a departure from her male contemporaries who rarely represented women as subjects in their own right, but as subordinate to the interests, needs or desires of a male-dominated social and cultural order. Feminist theatre criticism has since paid attention to Delaney as a pioneer of plays that represent women's lives and interests as central, rather than marginal, to modern British theatre and also to work by other women playwrights of the 1950s.[1] Looking back through this lens, *A Taste of Honey* and 1958 (rather than 1956) emerges as a critical year, marks the early stages of an alternative socially-aware and gender-aware theatre tradition.[2]

For example, Delaney's exploration of a mother and daughter relationship is one which prefigures or anticipates many of the maternal and filial discontents of the 1970s Women's Liberation Movement: generational conflict in mother–daughter relations, the maternal as women's biologically-driven 'destiny', or women's dual career' as mothers and workers. Jo's ambition and need to have a space or room of her own situate her firmly in a feminist tradition that challenges patriarchal ownership of women's lives, that cites the inequalities of a double standard of sexual morality in which, for women (unlike men), 'a taste of honey' can leave the bitter taste of an unwanted pregnancy and run the risk of being branded a 'little whore' (p. 62).

However, as a dramatist writing before the 1970s generation of feminist playwrights and practitioners, who represented these kinds of women's issues in their theatre and performances, Delaney had no community of women's theatre in which to situate her work. As the feminist theatre critic Sue-Ellen Case writes: 'Her [Jo's] isolation

---

[1] See Susan Bennett's essay, 'New Plays and Women's Voices in the 1950s', in Elaine Aston and Janelle Reinelt (eds), *Modern British Women Playwrights*, Cambridge: Cambridge University Press, 2000, pp. 38–52.
[2] See Lib Taylor's 'Early Stages: Women Dramatists 1958–68' in Trevor R. Griffiths and Margaret Llewellyn-Jones, *British and Irish Women Dramatists Since 1958*, Buckingham: Open University Press, 1993, pp. 9–25.

and suspension reflect Delaney's own historical situation as an isolated playwright, writing before the commencement of the feminist movement and its critique, but with the impulse towards staging the oppression and promise in the lived experiences of women.'[1] That impulse towards reflecting the 'oppression and promise' of women's lives is demonstrated in Delaney's socially-aware dramatisation of the 'lived experiences' of Helen and Jo as working-class women in the 1950s, which importantly counterpoints the received view of the decade as one of relative affluence and prosperity. These were the post-war years when people enjoyed to a greater or lesser extent the benefits of education, health and family care.[2] War-time austerity was becoming a thing of the past, giving way to economic growth, high employment and the opportunity to consume (especially by a new teen market). Delaney, however, depicts Helen and Jo as receiving none of these benefits. As John Russell Taylor observed, 'in almost every way the action might be taking place before the Welfare State was invented'.[3]

Just as mother and daughter fail to benefit from the new systems of health and social welfare, they also fall outside the (hetero)sexual configuration of the patriarchally conceived family. Conservative family values,[4] are alien to Jo's and Helen's social realities, where fathers are absent, or husbands (like Helen's Peter) are abusive, and the filthy stink of their urban neighbourhood is populated by an invisible chorus of uncared-for children. But in this, and in other ways, *A Taste of Honey* offers socially-aware views of family and of sexuality, and while critical reassessments of *Look Back in Anger* have pointed to the play's misogyny,[5] *A Taste of Honey*, by contrast, has been taken up and discussed as a play that points to a far more progressive understanding of social and sexual outsiders.

Surveying representations of homosexuality on stage, for example, Nicholas de Jongh credits *A Taste of Honey* as 'the first modern

[1] Sue-Ellen Case, 'The Power of Sex: English Plays by Women, 1958–1988, *New Theatre Quarterly*, August 1991, p. 239.
[2] The 1944 Butler Education Act introduced secondary education for all children. The National Health Service was established in 1948 and the Family Allowance system was introduced in 1945.
[3] John Russell Taylor, *Anger and After*, p. 133.
[4] Conservative family values were renewed through the coronation of the young Queen Elizabeth (1953) and a Conservative government that survived three general elections to remain in power throughout the 1950s.
[5] For further discussion of this point see Stephen Lacey, *British Realist Theatre: The New Wave in its Context 1956–1965*, London: Routledge, 1995, p. 2.

British play to depict a working-class homosexual'.[1] While there are ambiguities in the relationship between Jo and Geof as de Jongh acknowledges (the tensions of a friendship in which Geof is sometimes teased and laughed at by Jo on account of his sexuality, at the same time as he proves her most valuable and valued source of support), he nevertheless sees Jo's brief acceptance of Geof, a working-class girl befriending a gay man, as a 'new departure'.[2] Similarly, writing at the time of the play's production, Colin MacInnes observed, 'Shelagh Delaney's *A Taste of Honey* is the first English play I've seen in which a coloured man, and a queer boy, are presented as natural characters, factually without a nudge or shudder.'[3] While the return to the mother–daughter relationship in the ending of the play, which mirrors its opening, has disappointed some (feminist) critics looking for a more radical form of closure (if Geof, for example, had ultimately been the one to stay and queer the paternal role more thoroughly and completely through his homosexuality), it is in many ways an uneasy and ambiguous return, and a curious twist to the patriarchal tale of errant mothers, wives or daughters forced out of the family home: the mother thrown out of a 'respectable' home and marriage, instead finds refuge in the 'illegitimate' space of her daughter.

It is not only Delaney's social awareness that marks her play as progressive, but also its form. While for many critics Jimmy Porter's revolutionary anger has come to feel as dated, antiquated and as conservative as the play's form of realism, *A Taste of Honey* has much to recommend it in terms of its Brechtian-inflected, popular and interrogative style. Formally, the play reflects the collaboration between Delaney and Joan Littlewood's Theatre Workshop, and Littlewood's engagement with the popular traditions of music hall, *commedia dell' arte*, and with a Brechtian, political theatre tradition. Littlewood's concern that 'theatre must be in the present tense', and that for theatre 'to fulfil its social purpose it is contemporary and vital material which must make up the dramaturgy'[4] is thoroughly reflected in both the content *and* form of *A Taste of Honey*. Formally, Russell Taylor described *A*

[1] Nicholas de Jongh, *Not in Front of the Audience: Homosexuality on Stage*, London: Routledge, 1992, pp. 91–2.

[2] Ibid., p. 93.

[3] Colin MacInnes, *England, Half English*, London: Macgibbon & Kee, 1961, p. 205.

[4] Joan Littlewood, 'Plays for the People', *World Theatre*, 8(4), 1959–60, p. 286.

Taste of Honey (with Littlewood's input) as 'magnified realism',[1] though arguably broken realism is more accurate, where realism is broken, interrupted, interrogated by the characters' worlds, by the breaking-up of scenes through the use of music or dance, and by a style of dialogue that refuses to create a hermetically-sealed world, but which instead reports and questions – engaging the audience as it does so. To be interrogative is to ask the questions, not give the answers, as Delaney fully and firmly illustrated in the closing moments of her play, as Helen, who admonishes Jo with the line, 'I don't know what's to be done with you, I don't really', then breaks the fictional world with a question directly addressed to the audience, 'I ask you, what would you do?' (p. 87). Stylistically the play prefigures the gestic-feminist dramaturgy of the 1970s; of, for example, Caryl Churchill's Brechtian-feminist explorations of sexual politics in *Cloud Nine* (1979) or women's oppression in *Vinegar Tom* (1976). While critics obsessed over how much of the play was Delaney's and how much was Littlewood's, time has taught us to recognise the social, political and theatrical value of collaborative authorship and of collective, ensemble playing – this especially at the feminist time of collective, political theatre-making and staging.

During the last fifty years, adaptations of *A Taste of Honey* for film and radio, and the countless stage revivals, nationally and internationally, attest to the play's significance in twentieth-century British theatre. Although, at the risk of stating the obvious, times have changed dramatically (in all senses of the word) since 1958, there are moments in Delaney's play which *feel* highly contemporary. As Jo and Geof express their desire to be 'unique', 'unusual' (p. 50), they give expression to desiring beyond the norms and constraints of their gender-defined roles or sexual identities. That was a unique and transgressive wish back in 1958. As it resonates with our contemporary concerns for more progressive and less socially and sexually oppressive views and attitudes, both on and off stage, it also singles out *A Taste of Honey* as a play of its time and ahead of its time.

Elaine Aston
Lancaster, 2008

---

[1] Russell Taylor, *Anger and After*, p. 132.

Shelagh Delaney

1939   Shelagh Delaney was born in Salford, Lancashire. At eleven years old she failed to pass the examination that would allow her to go to a grammar school, and went to Broughton Secondary School. Later she showed herself intelligent enough to have the opportunity of being moved to a grammar school as a 'late developer' but by this time she had lost interest in academic progress, and did not go on to higher education.

1955   After leaving school she worked in various jobs in Salford – salesgirl, cinema usherette and photographer's laboratory assistant.

1958   Her first play, *A Taste of Honey*, was accepted by Joan Littlewood for production by the Theatre Workshop Company, then approaching the height of its fame. The play opened on 27 May at the Theatre Royal, Stratford, East London.

1959   *A Taste of Honey* transferred to the West End of London on 10 February for a long run. For this play she received the Foyle's New Play Award and an Arts Council Bursary.

1960   Her second play, *The Lion in Love*, was staged at the Belgrade Theatre, Coventry and then at the Royal Court Theatre, London. *A Taste of Honey* was put on in New York.

1961   *A Taste of Honey* won the New York Drama Critics Circle Award.

1962   She wrote the screenplay for the film version of *A Taste of Honey* with Tony Richardson (who also directed), and gained the British Film Academy Award and the Robert Flaherty Award for the screenplay.

1963   Her collection of short stories, *Sweetly Sings the Donkey*, was published, and *The Lion in Love* was produced in New York. She won the Encyclopaedia Britannica Award.

1966   She wrote the screenplay for the film *The White Bus*, directed by Lindsay Anderson.

1968   She wrote the screenplay for the film *Charley Bubbles*, directed by Albert Finney.

1969 The *Charley Bubbles* screenplay won the Writers Guild Award.

1970 Her television play *Did Your Nanny Come From Bergen?* was broadcast.

1974 She wrote the television play *St Martin's Summer*.

1977 *The House That Jack Built*, a six-part BBC-TV play, was broadcast.

1979 She adapted *The House That Jack Built* for stage and it was performed at the Cubiculo in New York directed by Will MacAdam. *Find Me First* was broadcast on BBC-TV.

1980 Her radio play *So Does The Nightingale* was broadcast.

1981 Roundabout Theatre staged a revival of *A Taste of Honey* off-Broadway directed by Tony Tanner. The production was named Critics' Choice in the *New York Times*. Amanda Plummer received the John Willes Theatre World Award for the Most Promising New Talent for her performance as Jo. The play transferred to the Century Theatre on Broadway. Shelagh Delaney wrote the radio play *Don't Worry About Matilda*.

1982 She wrote the screenplay for the film *Dance With A Stranger*.

1983 *Don't Worry About Matlda* was broadcast.

1985 The screenplay for *Dance With A Stranger* won the Prix Populaire at the Cannes Film Festival. Shelagh Delaney was made a Fellow of the Royal Society of Literature.

1987 She wrote the screenplay for the film *Love Lessons*.

1990 She wrote the screenplay for the film *The Railway Station Man*, directed by Michael Whyte.

2000 *For Being a Boy* and *Sweetly Sings the Donkey* were broadcast on BBC Radio 4.

2003 *Out of the Pirate's Playhouse* and *Tell Me a Film* were broadcast on BBC Radio.

2004 *Country Life* and *Baloney Said Salome* were broadcast on BBC Radio. *A Taste of Honey* was broadcast on BBC Radio 3 directed by Polly Thomas, and there was a stage revival at Theatre Royal, York.

2005 A stage revival of *A Taste of Honey* by Tag, at the Citizens Theatre, Glasgow.

2006 Stage revivals of *A Taste of Honey* included productions at Sheffield Crucible Theatre; Theatre Royal, Nottingham; Richmond Theatre, Surrey, and Oldham Coliseum.

2007 *A Taste of Honey* revived at the Lowry, Salford.

Plot and structure

Act One Scene One

Helen and her teenage daughter Jo are moving into a shabby flat. Within a few minutes we learn that they have little money, that they live off Helen's 'immoral earnings' (the money given her by her lovers), that Helen drinks a lot, and that she and Jo have a hostile rather than affectionate relationship. As they settle in, Helen's surprise at some of Jo's drawings both suggests Jo's talent and originality, and show Helen's previous lack of interest in or knowledge of her daughter; and Jo, rejecting the idea that she should go to art school, blames Helen for disrupting her education by moving her constantly from school to school: she now only wants to leave school and earn enough money to get away from Helen.

Once this exposition of their past lives and present relationship has been established, Peter, Helen's boyfriend comes in – Jo assumes that Helen has moved here to escape from him, but we never learn why. Younger than Helen, he had not realised she was old enough to have a daughter of Jo's age, but nonetheless asks Helen, half-jokingly, to marry him.

By the time Peter leaves, most of the basic information about the two women characters has been given, and most of this has arisen naturally in the course of the dialogue.

Act One Scene Two

This scene falls into four main parts, in which Jo's meetings with her boyfriend alternate with her confrontations with Helen, so that we see how Helen's indifference makes Jo seize happiness elsewhere. It begins out of doors where Jo is walking home with her black boyfriend. During a lighthearted conversation he asks her to marry him, and she agrees, although he is in the navy and will be away on his ship for six months before they can marry. He gives Jo a ring which she hangs round her neck under her clothes so that Helen will not see it. We also learn that Jo is going to start a part-time job in a pub. The next sequence takes place inside the flat, without change of scene or pause for change of scenery, and Helen tells Jo she is going to marry Peter. Almost immediately Peter enters, and a dialogue that is frequently hostile begins between the three: instead of only Jo and Helen sparring between themselves, a more complex pattern evolves, with Jo attacking both Helen and Peter, Helen alternately attacking and defending both the other two, and Peter cajoling Helen while ignoring or criticising Jo. Jo is genuinely upset at the thought of Peter marrying her mother, but also pesters and provokes him in an effort to antagonise him even more.

After Helen and Peter leave, Jo weeps, and is consoled by her boyfriend. Since Helen is going to leave her on her own at Christmas as usual, Jo invites the boy to stay with her, although she has a feeling that she will never see him again.

A pause and darkness mark the passage of time to Helen's wedding day after Christmas. Because Jo is in bed with a bad cold she cannot go to the wedding, and Helen is able to see the ring hanging round her neck under her pyjamas. She scolds Jo violently for thinking of marrying so young, with one of her occasional bursts of real feeling and concern for her daughter. Asked by Jo about her real father, Helen explains that she had been married very young to a man who had no interest at all in sex, and that her first sexual experience was with the 'not very bright' man who was Jo's father – he had been not an idiot but 'a bit – retarded'. She then hurries off to her wedding.

Act Two Scene One
Several months later Jo is living alone in the flat, working in a shoe shop by day and in a bar in the evenings to pay the rent. She is pregnant, and her boyfriend has not come back to her. She returns to the flat from a fair with Geof, an art student, who has possibly been thrown out of his lodgings because his landlady thought he was a homosexual. Jo offends him by her insensitive mocking curiosity about his sexual habits, but apologises and asks him to stay. Geof shows concern for Jo's problems, and they establish a friendly joking relationship. Darkness marks the passing of some months. Jo is next seen irritable and depressed by her pregnancy, with Geof patiently consoling her. Then, seeking reassurance from her in turn, he kisses her and begs her to marry him; Jo says that although she likes him she could not marry him. Nonetheless Geof refuses to leave, saying he cares so much about Jo that he would sooner be dead than away from her. At this point Helen arrives, and though Geof tries to conceal the fact that he has sent for her, Jo guesses and is as angry with him as she is with Helen. Whenever

Geof intervenes in the quarrel between the women he is attacked by one or the other or both – culminating in a chase round the flat. As Helen is offering Jo money, Peter comes in, very drunk, and insults the other three. He evidently no longer cares for Helen – he has been away with another woman – and takes back the money Helen has given, contradicting her offer of a home to Jo. He leaves insisting that Helen come with him; after a moment of indecision she runs after him.

Act Two Scene Two
More time has passed and Jo's baby is due. She and Geof seem happy; he reassures her that Helen was probably mistaken or exaggerating or both about the mental deficiency of Jo's father. Geof has bought a doll for her to 'practise' on but Jo flings it away because it is the wrong colour: she assumes her baby will be black like its father. Her outburst against the baby, motherhood and womanhood is shortlived, however, and she and Geof are about to have a peaceful tea when Helen reappears, this time with all her luggage. She has apparently been thrown out by Peter, plans to stay with Jo, and in the course of overwhelming Jo with presents and advice, is very rude to Geof and obviously intends to make him leave. Jo defends him, but while she is asleep, Geof decides to go, partly because Helen is so forceful, partly because he knows that Jo won't be able to cope with both him and Helen. When Jo wakes, Helen pretends that Geof is out shopping still, and is kind and helpful when Jo's first labour pains start. However, she is shattered to learn that the baby's father was black, and rushes out for a drink, saying she will come back. Jo is left alone, thinking quite happily about Geof and his gentleness.

Commentary

Characters

The Women

Jo. Although Helen is such an unsatisfactory mother, she has affected Jo's life and character very profoundly. Jo's insecurity and self-reliance both come from Helen's neglect. Jo has never been able to rely on Helen, so she is unwilling to rely on anyone else – she foresees that her boyfriend will not return to her, though he says he will, and she is reluctant to allow Geof to look after her, later suggesting that he leaves. On the other hand, because she cannot bring herself to rely on others, she feels that she has to be self-sufficient and cope with all her problems herself. 'You're nothing to me', she tells Geof. 'I'm everything to myself' (p. 57). This mixture of insecurity and confidence extends to her view of life in general: 'it's chaotic – a bit of love, a bit of lust and there you are. We don't ask for life, we have it thrust upon us' (p. 71); and to her own life in particular. Like her drawings, as Geof says, her life has no 'rhythm, design or purpose'. The title of the play applies more to Jo than to the other characters, though all of them seize what momentary sweetness life offers them: but Jo is less optimistic about the future than the others – to her boyfriend's plans she says 'I'll probably never see you again. I know it' (p. 38). Her reply to the question 'Afraid someone'll see us?' is 'I don't care' (p. 22), and her boyfriend comments: 'You mean it too. You're the first girl I've met who really didn't care (p. 23).

Without expecting very much from life or other people, she is still willing to enjoy the present moment – joking and fantasising with her boyfriend or with Geof. There is perhaps some escapism in the childlike games and rhymes she retreats into – a carefree state she had never known as a child. Her independence makes her work hard to pay the rent, but she is unwilling to accept the responsibility of having the baby – it would be 'terrible' to have an abortion (p. 49), but she deliberately refuses to think about how she is going to cope with it. At one extreme moment, she cries

I'll bash its brains out. I'll kill it. I don't want his baby, Geof. I don't want to be a mother. I don't want to be a woman. (p. 75)

She will be trapped in one role, and her independence will be gone. Symbolising this is Jo's fear of the dark – of the unkown, of uncertainty – which applies specifically to the dark inside houses, associated with people and with being enclosed. She doesn't mind the dark *outside*, because she 'doesn't care' about the great open world and what life may or may not happen to bring.

For a lot of the play, Jo exists in relation to Helen, even when Helen is not present. Jo continually refers things to Helen, seeing things in relation to her mother's existence. Because she blames Helen for failing as a mother, she interprets other people's lives in the same way:

JO: . . . and look at those filthy children.
GEOF: It's not their fault.
JO: It's their parents' fault. There's a little boy over there and his hair, honestly, it's walking away. And his ears. Oh! He's a real mess! He never goes to school. He just sits on that front doorstep all day. I think he's a bit deficient.

The children's voices die away. A tugboat boots.

His mother ought not to be allowed.
GEOF: Who?
JO: His mother. Think of all the harm she does, having children. (p. 54)

(And as Helen has claimed that Jo's father was mentally deficient, Jo is here blaming her mother for her own imperfect existence.)

As Jo is growing up, she also shows a sense of rivalry with Helen. She makes a few brief attempts to flirt with Peter – 'Do you fancy me?' (p. 32) – and questions her boyfriend about his reaction to Helen: 'Do you fancy her?' and 'Do you think Helen's beautiful?' and 'Am I like her?' (p. 37) concluding 'Good. I'm glad nobody can see a resemblance between us' (p. 38). Later, when Geof warns 'If you don't watch it, you'll turn out exactly like her . . . In some ways you are already, you know' (p. 72), she reacts by pushing his hands away in rejection and annoyance. Yet when Helen reminisces about 'my first job, in a tatty little pub', Jo asks 'What would you say if I got a job in a pub?' (pp. 12–13) and eventually she *does* get her first job in a pub too.

If Jo's feelings for Helen were of simple dislike, or indifference, there would be less tension and variety in their relationship: the remnants of a child's dependence on its mother appear in Jo's sudden, childish attack on Peter:

Suddenly she attacks him, half-laughing, half-crying.

Jo: You leave me alone. And leave my mother alone too. (p. 30)

Helen rightly comments on this childish possessiveness when she complains 'She's jealous ... Can't bear to see me being affectionate with anybody' (p. 19) – and Jo is still very young; school-leaving age was then fifteen, so she is unlikely to be the seventeen-year-old she claims. Jo even boasts of Helen 'No, whatever else she might be, she isn't prejudiced against colour' (p. 23) – wrongly, as it turns out. But this possessiveness and defence of Helen remain to explain Jo's feeling of rejection; as she says, Helen has always had 'so much love for everyone else, but none for me' (p. 72) – and this had made Jo selfish as well as independent.

So Jo's repeated insistence on her own special individuality, and her denial of womanhood and of love, are, like her actions, ways of trying to detach herself from Helen's dominating personality – and ironically she does this by assuming those of Helen's characteristics which have so damaged her.

Helen. About Helen, Shelagh Delaney herself said, 'The mother is not a prostitute, I have nowhere said that she is – would she have kept her daughter with her if she had been? She is just a woman who enjoys life and goes about it in her own way.' The bad effect she has on Jo – and on Geof – is not due to malice or cruelty, but to sheer lack of thought about other people. A scatterbrained woman who can never find her hat or shoes, she says 'I don't forget things: it's just that I can't remember anything' (p. 64). But as Jo stresses by using much the same words each time – 'You always have to rush off into things. You never think' (p. 9), and 'You never think. That's your trouble' (p. 43) – this extends to more serious matters like choosing a flat and, most important, having 'a little love affair that lasted five minutes' with the 'retarded' man who was Jo's father (p. 43).

This is Helen's attitude to life, in fact. When Jo tells her that she is not sulking but thinking, Helen replies, 'Well, don't think. It doesn't do you any good' (p. 44). Like Jo, she does not calculate her future. As John Russell Taylor says:

Helen, too, is in her way a realist: she will try various means of escape, but never with any great conviction that they will work, and when things go wrong, as with her marriage, she is not really surprised. (*Anger and After*, p. 132)

The contrast between her practical advice to Jo and her resignation to the whims of fate in her own case appears neatly in her recommendation:

> There's two w's in your future. Work or want, and no Arabian Knight can tell you different. We're all at the steering wheel of our own destiny. Careering along like drunken drivers. I'm going to get married. (p. 29)

This one speech contains a magnificent mound of contradictions. 'Work or want' is a cliché of down-to-earth advice from mother to daughter. Yet the idea that there is some real choice to be made is undermined by her suggestion that we have as much control over our lives as a drunken driver has over his car. Helen then provides a perfect demonstration of how little control she has over her own life by announcing out of the blue that she's going to get married – evidently a spur-of-the-moment decision. The clever and articulate self-expression of this speech – and Helen has a good vocabulary – shows both her evident intelligence and her apparent inability to apply it to her own career.

Helen does have a few moments of apparently real affection for Jo, as in her concern about Jo's engagement 'Oh Joe, you're only a kid. Why don't you learn from my mistakes? It takes you half your life to learn from your own' (p. 41); or, learning of Jo's pregnancy, 'I haven't been able to sleep for thinking about you since he came round to our house' (p. 64); or in her support and reassurance when Jo's labour pains start. These however are pushed aside in Helen's determination to enjoy life: she tells Jo 'I never thought about you! It's a funny thing, I never have done when I've been happy' (p. 81). And as this admission shows, she is not hypocritical about her shortcomings: 'Have I ever laid claim to being a proper mother?' (p. 35). However when she asks Jo 'You've never had a boyfriend, have you?', which even the most indifferent mother would be likely to know already, this may be the author rather clumsily trying to disguise necessary information as dialogue, not Helen's lack of observation. On the other hand her later question 'Are you afraid of the dark?' which equally she must know already (as Jo comments 'You know I am' (p. 21)) is an example of Helen being deliberately annoying, if not cruel, to pay Jo back for being rude to Peter – but otherwise, if not provoked, her attitude is easy-going, with no hints of gratuitous hostility or sadism.

On Helen's side, it may be said that she has some motive for rejecting a mother's role herself, for it was Jo's birth, in revealing Helen's unfaithfulness, that made her husband divorce her – 'that was your fault' (p. 28) she tells Jo. Yet Helen is not on the whole one to bear malice, and it is more likely to be Jo's nuisance value in hampering her freedom – inasmuch as she does so – that provokes Helen's bursts of irritation. Helen is not inclined to restrain her irritation, any more than any other feeling – as appears in her exclamatory style of dialogue: 'Oh!' appears over and over in her speeches – and it is this readiness to demonstrate her feelings that makes her such an exuberant and powerful character, and in turn makes it so hard for her daughter to become truly independent of her.

The Men

> When I started this play I had only two people in it – the mother and daughter. Then I realized there had to be other characters so that these two could reveal themselves more fully. It built up on its own from that.

So Shelagh Delaney added further dimensions to the mother-daughter relationship. Helen's attractiveness is confirmed by Peter, Jo's ability to dominate develops in her friendship with Geof, and her affectionate and generous nature, dammed up by Helen, is revealed in the brief interchanges with her boyfriend.

Peter. John Russell Taylor thought that all the characters were difficult to judge merely by reading the text, without the additional expression and meaning put in by the actors, and he found this particularly so with the character of Peter. Would it be possible for an actor to make Peter a powerfully charming man? As a 'brash car salesman' he must habitually turn on his charm to manipulate people and make money, but his bursts of temper and his comic drunkenness ('*he falls into the kitchen, singing*', p. 65) seem to invite us to laugh *at* him rather than *with* him, and suggest that he is by no means in control. Even so, like the other men his character is only sketched in during his three brief appearances: at first he is almost singleminded – except for a rival interest in drink – in his sexual obsession with Helen, and his marrying her seems as impulsive and unwise as most people's actions in this play. Later he has tired of Helen and is very drunk, but we don't learn whether either of these facts has caused the other, or if they are coincidental.

His character is far from amiable, yet he seems to exist less as a personality in his own right than as a catalyst in the relationship between Helen and Jo, causing them to reveal more about their feelings for each other.

The Boyfriend. Jo's black boyfriend, who she says is called Jimmy, appealed to her 'because he could sing and he was so tender' (p. 75). He gives Jo the tenderness she has wanted but never had from her mother. Another quality is his lightheartedness. He is always joking: 'Honey, you've got to stop eating', he tells her. 'We're saving up to get married' (p. 25). Though like Peter he eventually leaves never to return, he seems sincere at the time when he says 'I will come back' (p. 39). Again, his character and motives are not developed for their own sake. In one sense, he is presented as a 'typical man' – he is 'only after one thing' (p. 39) and deserts her when he gets it, leaving her literally holding the baby. But in another sense, both he and Jo are jokily aware of all this and accept it willingly. There is even a suspicion that Jo is all the more attracted to him precisely because he is a sailor (who can only offer a very impermanent relationship) and because he is black (which she knows will scandalise her mother, even though she pretends it won't).

Geof. A more serious character than the other two men, he shows more responsibility in thinking about Jo's future, making practical arrangements for her to earn a little money retouching photographs, and trying to get some support for her from Helen. But though much of his dialogue consists of more serious speeches, patient argument and reassurance of Jo, he too jokes and laughs with her, as in their 'We're unique . . . Young . . . Unrivalled . . . Smashing!' sequence (pp. 50–1). Geof's homosexual tendencies are hinted at in Jo's apparently correct guess that his landlady has found him with a man and so evicted him (p. 47). His feeling for Jo is very strong – 'I'd sooner be dead than away from you' (p. 59) – but it does not seem to be a sexual attraction: he kisses her and asks her to marry him, but when he makes his 'rather be dead' speech, Jo goes to lie on her bed, probably consciously encouraging him to make love to her, but he does not. She later reminds him of this and points out to him 'And you didn't go and follow me, did you? . . . You see, it's not marrying love between us, thank God' (p. 76). Jo seems to derive security from the very fact that Geof is not sexually attracted to her: this is why she can play games with him and why she can flirt with him without danger. He is a cross between a husband and a mother, but he does not make the sexual and emotional demands on her that they would. So Jo feels safe with him.

Unfortunately it is his very gentleness, which Jo appreciates, that makes him unable to stand up to Helen – he is easily cowed by her rudeness. His is the most consistent affection Jo finds in the play, but it is his unselfish affection in the end which causes him to leave rather than upset Jo by keeping up a running battle with Helen.

Themes

> My title, *A Taste of Honey* – which everybody at one time in their lives experiences – comes from the Bible where Jonathan says to Saul, 'I did but taste a little honey with the end of the rod that was in mine hand, and lo I must die.'

All the characters in the play do indeed have their period of happiness – their 'taste of honey' – though not all of them have to suffer for it afterwards. We do not know about Jo's boyfriend, but Helen and Peter seem to relinquish their happiness with resignation and return more or less willingly to the status quo. It is Jo, and to some extent Geof, who find themselves in the end suffering for what they have enjoyed – Jo in the problems of having the baby, and Geof in losing his unforeseen relationship with Jo.

The play 'has no "ideas" which can be isolated and considered as such apart from their dramatic context' suggests John Russell Taylor, and it is true that there is no clear-cut message here. Nonetheless certain ideas, such as that of the chance of happiness in everyone's life, and its value, do emerge unobtrusively through the action.

Linked with this is the question of the individual's dependence or lack of dependence on others. Should happiness be taken at someone else's expense, as in Helen's case? What if happiness involves dependence on another person, as in Geof's case? The issue of responsibility is central to Jo's relationship with her mother. As in the novels of Dickens, there is a pattern of failed or substitute parents, which shows that the normal parental responsibilities are not functioning properly. Helen herself is a bad mother, and Jo is to be a mother but rejects the role, at least at times. It is a commonplace of popular psychology to say that dislike of milk (especially with the skin on it) symbolises rejection of one's mother: Jo dislikes milk, and interestingly both her boyfriend and Geof, who give her the care and affection lacking in her mother, try to make her drink glasses of milk. Geof is mocked by Jo for being more maternal than she is – it is he who makes baby clothes, organises the wicker cradle and buys the baby book and the baby doll. Even Helen's relationship with Peter is ambiguous: 'Listen, love, I'm old enough to be your mother' she tells him and he replies, petting her 'Now you know I like this mother and son relationship' (p. 18). But by the end of the play he compares himself to Oedipus, 'the chappie who married his mother by mistake' (p. 65).

Yet by the end of the play all the characters have separated again and disengaged from their relationships and responsibilities. Jo's boyfriend never comes back, Geof has been ousted by Helen, and Helen's new solicitude for her daughter is so shaken by the news that the baby's father is black that she too disappears, even if only temporarily, just as Jo's labour pains are beginning. Jo is left completely alone with the prospect of childbirth before her, but she is not distraught or depressed – she is 'smiling a little to herself'. Like the 'little miss' of the rhyme she recites, she is alone amidst squalor and poverty, yet her carefree independence is a 'blessing' to her. But although the play ends with a prospective birth, usually a sign of hope, Jo's life has been so battered by the insecurity, poverty and depressing conditions she has known, that a feeling of nightmare recurs throughout the action – the frighteningly dark flat is surrounded by Cemetery and Slaughterhouse. Jo's bulbs die, her father is dead (and her inability to face the idea of death is clear from her asking 'why?' not 'how?'). Her wry humour often gives way to depression, and there is a fear of inherited madness lurking in the back of her mind after Helen's remarks on her 'retarded' father. Her fear of darkness suggests this too, and the threatening aspects of all relationships are emphasised in the various black attributes of the men characters – the boyfriend's skin, Peter's eye-patch, Geof's shirt. This undercurrent of awareness of the darker aspects of life gives depth to the characters' ability to remain buoyant and, in Shelagh Delaney's own words, to 'take in their stride whatever happens to them and remain cheerful'.

Comedy

In spite of the serious themes treated in the play, a lot of it is very funny, and the action often takes the form of classic comedy routines, traditional in music hall and variety show. So the very opening lines of the play.

HELEN: Well! This is the place.
JO: And I don't like it. (p. 7)

set up the two characters as comic sparring partners, with Helen as the voluble, excitable one and Jo as the sardonic, wise-cracking one, constantly deflating Helen's extravagant statements as when Helen claims 'My figure hasn't changed an inch since I was eighteen' and Jo replies 'I hope I'm luckier with mine' (p. 30). Similarly, like a couple on a comic postcard, Peter pursues Helen who keeps evading him – the humour lies in his single-minded, predictable but ingenious persistence and her equally predictable rebuffs. Most obviously comic is the three-cornered quarrel between Helen, Jo and Geof when Helen first comes back to offer help. It is interesting to follow the ebb and flow of antagonism – the abrupt switches of complaint from one direction to another are comic in themselves, as the bystander suddenly becomes the target, to his amazement: sometimes, as when Geof intervenes to defend Jo, both the others turn on him together, united for a moment in exasperation. The visual slapstick of the comic chase adds to the verbal battle: 'Let me get hold of her' (p. 62) cries Helen, as Geof, trying to restrain her, appeals back and forth to each of them: 'Please Jo, Helen, Jo, please!' And extra comic effect is achieved when Geof's temper breaks just as the two women pause for breath, so that he is left yelling 'Will you stop shouting you two?' (p. 63) into complete silence.

Peter's second act appearance marks his change of comic role from persistent lover to comic drunk, falling over things, singing taglines from songs, being more uninhibited with his vivid insults than when sober and restrained by Helen. Catastrophe is one of the traditional materials of comedy, and Peter contributes by 'falling into the kitchen' where almost at once 'There is a loud crash' (p. 65). A similarly broad comic use of off-stage noises occurs when Jo is in the kitchen trying to light the gas cooker and Helen asks 'Did you find it?', and there is a 'Loud bang' before Jo replies with superfluous understatement, 'Yes' (p. 10).

But the majority of the comedy of the play comes from the dialogue and can to a great extent be appreciated from reading the text, Jo deflates Helen's exaggerations and pretensions, either with short criticisms, or more elaborately sarcastic comments, as when she remarks on Peter and Helen, who are obviously lovers, thinking of buying an engagement ring which is supposed to mark an early stage in a relationship: 'I should have thought that their courtship had passed the stage of symbolism' (p. 20). Helen, besides humorous exaggeration, can herself deflate expectations with an anti-climax. Her second speech in the play shows this fundamental comic pattern: 'When I find somewhere for us to live I have to consider something far more important than your feelings . . .' and she pauses while we wonder what powerful and amazing motive this can be, but then she adds briefly 'the rent!' (p. 7). She will also occasionally use unexpectedly long and impressive words for a fairly ordinary meaning, as 'The extent of my credulity always depends on the extent of my alcoholic intake' (p. 34). The comic effect is doubled when she uses equally elaborate terms to tell Peter that she only puts up with him being there because he will be gone soon: 'The only consolation I can find in your immediate presence is your ultimate absence' (p. 17), to which Peter at once replies 'In that case I'll stay', Not only are his simple words a comic contrast with hers, but he is taking, or pretending to take, her words in exactly the opposite sense to their real meaning. A great deal of the comic effect of the dialogue comes from Shelagh Delaney's ability to capture the way people actually talk, particularly their tendency to jump from one subject to another in the middle of a speech. For instance:

> HELEN: I said nobody asked you to come. Oh my God! I'll
> have to have a dose of something. My head's swimming.
> Why did you? (p. 17).

How the play came to be written

The Author's Intentions

One of the best-known facts about Shelagh Delaney herself is that she wrote *A Taste of Honey* when she was only eighteen. And this was without being a precocious intellectual. She had failed to pass the eleven-plus exam to go to a grammar school, and though she was a 'late-developer' and eventually transferred to a grammar school and took O-levels, she no longer had any interest in continuing academic education and left school to take a number of jobs, including shop assistant and usherette. But, she says, 'All the time I intended to write' (Kitchin, *Mid-Century Drama*, p. 167).

> Why a drama, rather than a novel or poetry? Because, according to her own account, she saw Rattigan's *Variation on a Theme* on tour and thought that if this was drama, she could do better herself. Unlike many other people who have thought the same, however, she set about doing something practical to find out whether she could or not, and the result was *A Taste of Honey*. (Taylor, *Anger and After*, p. 131)

Actually she told Laurence Kitchin that she had started it as a
novel, but changed it to a play after seeing the Rattigan. To her, the
polite drawing-room comedy, which still at this time was the staple
diet available to the theatre-goer, was unrealistic – it 'depicts safe,
sheltered, cultured lives in charming surroundings – not life as the
majority of ordinary people know it'. She herself put a high
priority on giving a picture of the vitality of those who, because of
their lack of money, privilege and amenities, have to struggle
actively to cope with all the problems that arise from their
deprivation. Delaney: 'I had strong ideas about what I wanted to
see in the theatre. We used to object to plays where factory workers
come cap in hand and call the boss "Sir". Usually North Country
people are shown as gormless whereas in actual fact they are very
alive and cynical.' Their life, she felt, produced not depression but
resilience: 'No one in my play despairs. Like the majority of people
they take in their stride whatever happens to them and remain
cheerful', and she added 'I see the theatre as a place where you
should go not only to be entertained but where the audience has
contact with *real* people, people who are *alive*'.

But the critic John Russell Taylor, whose book *Anger and After*
provides the best contemporary assessment of the playwrights of
Shelagh Delaney's generation, has doubts about how 'real' these
'real' people are:

> None of the characters looks outward at life beyond the closed
> circle of the stage world; they all live for and in each other, and
> finally the rest, even Helen, seem to exist only as incidentals in
> Jo's world, entering momentarily into her dream of life and
> vanishing when they have no further usefulness for it ... Even
> in its final form the play is still intensely introspective, still very
> much the acting out in dramatic terms of a young girl's fantasies.
> (pp. 133–136)

Joan Littlewood, Theatre Workshop and the First Production

Shelagh Delaney noticed a newspaper account of a conflict between
the Theatre Workshop company and the Lord Chamberlain, who at
that time had the power to censor plays before they were
performed and to have material cut out or altered if he felt it was
not acceptable. With her own strong views on presenting reality
without cuts or alterations, she took an interest in Theatre
Workshop's stand, and sent her play there, where it was accepted.
Theatre Workshop was a company set up after the war by the
famous director Joan Littlewood, and after touring Britain for

several years, it had settled in 1953 at the Theatre Royal, Stratford, in East London (no connection with Shakespeare's Stratford-upon-Avon). Though at first distinguished for productions of classic plays, old and new, it then gained a reputation for discovering new original works, beginning with Brendan Behan's *The Quare Fellow* in 1956. Joan Littlewood made her company what it was by discussion with her actors, by training in movement and singing, by requiring research from the actors into the background of plays – not only unusual in itself in that era, but unusual in the great amount of time the company was expected to put into these activities. Work on the many of the new plays, including *A Taste of Honey*, began with improvisation – the actors invented new scenes, situations and lines which were related to those in the original script, and which were sometimes incorporated into the author's script in the final production. John Russell Taylor's understanding of the process was that:

> almost every new play which was produced by the company under her rule passed through endless transformations in rehearsal – so much so that she compares the work of the actors in them to that of the players in the *commedia dell' arte*, working on a basic text but improvising freely around it, sometimes with the author's aid, sometimes without it. (*Anger and After*, p. 121)

Avis Bunnage, who played Helen, described the early rehearsals of *A Taste of Honey:*

> My first reaction was that whoever wrote this needed a swift kick up the arse. We did a lot of improvisation. When we came to bits that didn't seem to work we ad-libbed round the ideas, made it up as we went along. We used things that were around, an aspidistra that someone had left on the stage became incorporated into the production. I said some of my lines to it. Joan gave us hell during rehearsals. She had us running from the stage to the paint bay and back over and over again, to give us a feeling of real tiredness. (Howard Goorney: *The Theatre Workshop Story*, Eyre Methuen, 1981, p. 109)

Frances Cuka, who played Jo, qualified this picture slightly:

> There was a considerable amount of rewriting but most of the best bits were Shelagh's. We did a lot of improvisation using the original dialogue. It was too long, of course, but I think Shelagh just wrote down what she felt without editing or cutting. Peter,

the mother's boyfriend came in for the most rewriting. Some
outrageous speeches of his were kept in because Joan said it was
a young girl's play and we mustn't wreck the flavour of it . . .
(*The Theatre Workshop Story*, p. 109)

John Russell Taylor compared the original and final scripts in detail
and agrees with Frances Cuka that, interestingly enough, the
original was 'not so radically different from the version finally
performed as most published comment would lead one to believe,'
although there was substantial rewriting of Peter's character from 'a
complete seventeen-year-old's dream figure of cosmopolitan
sophistication' (with, as a bonus, a hidden 'child-loving heart of
gold' that makes him offer a home to Jo and her baby) to the
seedy, ambiguous character of the final text. The ending also was
altered: originally Helen packed Jo off to hospital to have the baby,
and planned to take her home afterwards, leaving Geof forlorn. And
Geof had more overt revelations of his homosexuality.

These were changes of substance: in style the first production was
in 'Joan Littlewood's characteristic manner, a sort of magnified
realism in which everything is like life but somehow larger than life'
(*Anger and After*, p. 134), with 'the introduction of a few lines
addressed, music-hall style, straight at the audience, and the slight
fantastication involved in having the characters dance on and off to
music' (*Anger and After* p. 135–6). Possibly this style and
fantastication added more jollity to the play than its original mood
would have afforded, and made the characters seem even more
'cheerful' than Shelagh Delaney had intended.

Shelagh Delaney herself was not only very happy with the
production but didn't notice the changes until they were pointed
out to her: of Joan Littlewood she said 'I think she is a genius, the
greatest woman in the theatre today. She has taught me so much'.

Dramatic effectiveness

Many of the dramatic techniques touched on already, such as
structure, comic effects, dialogue and so on, are also to be found in
novels – novels after all need a structure, which can be episodic
with changes of characters and moods, and novels too can include
comedy and dialogue: these might still have been present if Shelagh
Delaney had continued to write *A Taste of Honey* as a novel. But
the dramatic effectiveness of the play is the quality which the
audience reacts to when it is performed, and therefore this
effectiveness can be of two kinds – what is there in the text, such as
these elements of structure, comedy etc., and what is brought out in

production by a particular director and company of actors. Many of the comic elements such as the quarrels and confrontations need to be seen to be fully appreciated, and these will change slightly when different actors take the parts. Even the comic dialogue makes its point more easily on stage, aided by the actor's tone of voice, timing and facial expression, which readers have to imagine for themselves.

On the other hand the individual structure of the play – how the situation is revealed (quickly and economically, in this case), what aspects are given importance, such as the Jo-Helen relationship, and what are passed over briefly, such as Jo's short period of happiness, the deliberately quiet conclusion – this can all be taken from the printed text. And the time structure of the second act, which moves from episode to episode with months passing in between, is spelled out in the stage directions for the *reader*, but happens without this clear explanation in *performance*. This helps give the 'dreamlike' effect that John Russell Taylor refers to. There is little reason in fact to divide the play into the conventional acts and scenes indicated in the text – the events flow in episodic sequence one after the other, the passing of time shown by such things as the progress of Jo's pregnancy. But again, though the changes of mood from episode to episode – as in Helen's breezy interruptions of harmony between Geof and Jo – are clear from the text, such changes can obviously be brought out more fully by differences in sound, tempo and movement.

As mentioned before, many of these episodes correspond to traditional music-hall routines or variety acts. A comedy duo (Helen and Jo) would be joined by a comic spiv (Peter) to make a slanging match for three. Later, a boy-girl act (Jo and Boyfriend) would be followed by a return of the comedy duo. And so on. This arrangement was emphasised in Joan Littlewood's production by giving the characters their own individual signature tunes to be played by the band as the characters enter and leave the stage. Comedians also tend to address the audience directly, and this too was incorporated into the play, particularly for the character of Helen:

> Instead of observing a distant ritual, they found themselves whisked up into the action. At the beginning of *A Taste of Honey*, for example, a more or less naturalistic sequence shows the mother and daughter together. Jo goes out to make some coffee, while the mother goes on talking to her. She turns her head quite casually, and suddenly she is talking directly to the

audience. (Marowitz and Trussler, eds. *Theatre at Work*, Methuen, 1967, p. 114)

However Helen's speeches *need* not be played that way. Because the dimension of performance can vary, it would be possible for a director to decide to cut out the music and on-stage band and stress the 'more or less naturalistic' side of the play. The sentences Helen addresses to the audience could just as well be addressed to no one in particular – it would fit perfectly with Helen's exclamatory style for her to appeal to the heavens or to the world in general.

Some directors of course change and distort a play until the effect is quite different from what the author intended: the value of Joan Littlewood's first production was that, while giving her own individual stamp to the performance, she was careful, as Frances Cuka said, to retain the original youthful flavour of the play – 'to bring out the best in an author's work while staying completely true to its spirit' (*Anger and After*, p. 136).

Social background: the fifties

By the late nineteen-fifties Britain had recovered from the shortages and rationing that were the aftermath of the war: rationing of sweets, meat, bacon, butter, cheese, tea, and sugar finally ended in 1952. The average wage almost doubled from £6 8s per week in 1950 to £112s6d in 1959; there was virtually full employment, and plenty of consumer goods in the shops; and the Welfare State, by providing medical, unemployment and other benefits, had removed people's fear of having to pay large and unforeseen sums of money in the event of illness or other misfortune. So to those in employment earning the average wage or more, without too many commitments and with access to consumer goods, this was the beginning of the era of affluence.

But not everyone was in this fortunate position, as Shelagh Delaney showed in her play. Housing was still scarce, many bomb sites still derelict, where houses destroyed in the war had not been rebuilt, and many people had to live in flats like Helen's even if, unlike Helen, they could have afforded something better. Nevertheless, there was an outcry against Shelagh Delaney's play – 'They think I have slandered Salford', she said – probably because those who were benefitting from this new tide of affluence resented the implication that all working-class Salford lived in squalor like Helen and Jo.

Related to this affluence was the increasing importance of teenagers. Obviously the rebellion of a younger generation against its elders is a phenomenon that is as old as mankind, but the new factor in the late 1950s was the higher earnings of the great majority of teenagers, so they had growing importance in the commercial world and were less subject to financial control by their elders. As Jo says: as soon as she gets a job, she'll be able to leave Helen and live her own life. Rejection of adult values and enthusiasm for a life-style that would be unique to their generation resulted in several phenomena, some of which have survived, others not, such as rock-'n'-roll, coffee bars, distinctive dress – the long hair and flamboyant clothes of the 'Teds' that Jo refers to were in defiant contrast to the unobtrusive suits and short hair of their elders.

It was the post-war Labour government that had removed the anxiety of the average working person about not being able to afford essential medical attention and so on, and this had seemed to herald a new, inspiring, transformed society, but by the late fifties affluence was, some thought, becoming an end in itself: people were earning more money in order to buy more things, and happiness was simply having more material possessions than the neighbours.

The younger generation of writers reacted against this; and the group labelled by the media the 'Angry Young Men', who included John Osborne and Colin Wilson, fiercely criticised the complacent and limited attitudes of their contemporaries – the hero of Osborne's play *Look Back in Anger* (1956), Jimmy Porter, became the symbol of this criticism. Plays and novels also began to appear written by very young writers – the new importance of youth meant that the novelty of being exceptionally youthful attracted immediate attention, regardless of the value of the work. As Kenneth Allsop commented:

> Lack of years carries a *cachet* whether you are drumming hell out of a mistuned guitar, writing a novel or just acting the jean-ager behind the bamboo curtain in your local *capuccino* shebeen. (*The Angry Decade*, Peter Owen, 1958, p. 133)

Shelagh Delaney was anxious not to be dismissed as a novelty of this kind:

> The fact that I am working-class and was only eighteen when I wrote the play is not what matters, and I get annoyed at critics who think it is good – or bad – because of things like that. I think my *work* is what should be considered, not myself.

She is in fact usually grouped with the 'New Wave' dramatists who were coming into prominence in the late fifties – John Osborne,

Arnold Wesker, John Arden, Harold Pinter, and others – not all of whom were 'angry' in a socially conscious way, but who were dramatically revolutionary in dealing with working-class characters in their homes and places of work, as opposed to the upper-class characters in their drawing-rooms who had dominated the English stage since the beginning of the century. With one or two exceptions, working-class characters had tended to be used for comic effect, or to make some special topical point. Here, on the other hand, were the New Wave dramatists using this background as a matter of course. This was true of *A Taste of Honey* and its characters:

> They accept their life and go on living, without making any too serious complaint about their lot; unlike Jimmy Porter and his followers, Jo is not angry, nor does she rail savagely and ineffectually against the others – authority, the Establishment, fate. In practice, she recognizes that her fate is in her own hands, and takes responsibility for the running of her own life without a second's thought – indeed, in almost every way the action might be taking place before the Welfare State was invented. (*Anger and After*, p. 133)

Shelagh Delaney was concerned with the reality that she knew existed outside the glossy affluent image of the advertisements: and because she was also concentrating on the individual's response to life, most of the more public and social issues that were important at this time are ignored. It was, for instance, the period of the 'Cold War' between America and Russia, during which America was pillorying Communists and Communist sympathisers – hence Jo is trying to shock Helen when she says 'We're communists too' (p. 62). Most important was the new threat of nuclear war. After the explosion of the first atom bomb in 1945, research on a hydrogen bomb began in 1950. A hydrogen nuclear 'device' was successfully exploded by the Americans in 1952, followed, unexpectedly quickly, by a Russian hydrogen bomb in 1953. The nuclear arms race had begun, with its prospect of destruction on a scale never imaginable before. Apart from a possible oblique reference when Geof asks, of Jo's sudden thoughts about death, 'What's frightened you? Have you been reading the newspapers?' (p. 71), there is nothing about this in the play. Yet perhaps the awareness of this new condition of life alters the way the characters look at the world; one commentator on the decade thinks it changed attitudes profoundly:

Indeed it is possible to see the fifties as a major psychological watershed in history – not the beginning of a new half-century but of a new planet. In the sense that the nineteenth century did not really end until 1914, so the twentieth century did not truly begin until at the earliest 1945, and possibly not until the bigger explosion of 1950 changed the facts of life for all to see. In between had been a No Man's Land and a No Man's Time of warfare and truce conducted according to left-over beliefs in competitive nationalism, in patriotism and in victory in just causes. All these suddenly became untenable, dissolving in the mushroom cloud. (Peter Lewis, *The Fifties*, Heinemann, 1978, pp. 7–8)

Reviews and reception

A Taste of Honey earned Delaney 'a considerable reputation with the critics and the theatregoing public,' commented John Russell Taylor, 'high sales for her published texts, and [. . .] a prompt film adaptation right on the heels of long and successful runs in the West End and on Broadway – all this by the time she was twenty-two.'[1] Look back at first theatre reviews or critical commentaries, and what you discover is that so many of these mix commentaries of the play with observations about Delaney, about her gender, age, class, or even her height (see Tynan's review extract below)! In brief, reviews and criticism are often characterised by a note of astonishment that someone of Delaney's age, class and gender could be the author of *A Taste of Honey*. Not all commentaries, however, patronise Delaney's writing success, as Colin MacInnes observed, 'It is, of course, wonderful that a woman of nineteen has written this play, but I must make it clear I think no note of condescension is permissible on account of Shelagh Delaney's age. The play lives in its own right entirely.'[2]

While Delaney's age, gender and class background formed one reviewing focus, another attended to the style of Littlewood's production. It is interesting to compare and contrast the following views of Lindsay Anderson (director and critic) and Kenneth Tynan (theatre critic). Anderson's view is one of praise, both for the playwright and Littlewood's production:

> One of the most extraordinary things about this play is its lack of bitterness, its instinctive maturity. This quality was emphasized by Joan Littlewood's production, which seemed to

[1] *Anger and After*, p. 130.
[2] Op. cit. pp. 205–6.

me quite brilliant. Driving the play along at breakneck pace, stuffing it with wry and humorous invention, she made sentimentalism impossible. The abandoning of the fourth wall, the sudden patches of pure music hall, panto-style, were daring, but completely justified by their success. No soppy 'identification' here; just the ludicrous, bitter-sweet truth, a shared story.[1]

Tynan, on the other hand, tempers praise with reservations about the production style:

At the Criterion there is *A Taste of Honey*, a first play by Shelagh Delaney, a Lancashire girl who is well over six feet tall and just over twenty years old. It deals joyfully with what might, in other hands, have been a tragic situation [. . .] I don't know that I like all of Miss Littlewood's production tricks; I don't see why the mother should address all her lines to the audience, like a vaudeville soloist, [. . .] All the same, we have here quite a writer, and quite a director.[2]

In brief, a comparison of this kind helps to show us how the reception of Delaney's play was also shaped by (mis)understandings of the play's staging by Littlewood and her Theatre Workshop.

It might be tempting to think, perhaps, that the gender bias of reviews can be accounted for, in part at least, as a reflection of the critical values and judgements of fifties theatre criticism, before feminist theatre criticism of the 1970s challenged the bias of the theatre canon and reviewing body, and generated a community of feminist theatre and women's playwriting. Except that more recently, in these so-called 'post-feminist' times, (gender) history appears to be repeating itself: the parallels drawn between the 1950s as the decade of 'angry young men' and the 1990s as a decade of angry new 'in-yer-face' theatre, with Osborne resurrected as *the* point of reference for looking back in anger, also positions a new generation of nineties writers as young, angry and *male*. Very few 'in-yer-facers' are women. The notable exception is the late Sarah Kane, and while the reception of Kane and Delaney is radically different in one way (given the notoriety attached to Kane's debut play *Blasted*, 1995), in another, they share the experience of having

[1] Lindsay Anderson, '*A Taste of Honey*', in Charles Marowitz, Tom Milkne and Owen Hale, (eds), *The Encore Reader*, London: Methuen, 1965, pp. 79–80.
[2] Kenneth Tynan, 'Summing-Up: 1959', in *Tynan on Theatre*, Harmondsworth: Pelican, 1964, pp. 88–9.

their work evaluated and critiqued on account of their relative inexperience as playwrights, their youth and their gender. To compare the reception of these debut plays and writers, despite the years that separate them, makes for an illuminating study.

Suggestions for further reading

Plays and novels from the fifties
(*with date of first publication and current paperback publisher*)

Kingsley Amis, *Lucky Jim*, 1954; Harmondsworth: Penguin
John Braine, *Room at the Top*, 1957; Harmondsworth: Penguin
John Osborne, *Look Back in Anger*, 1956; London: Faber
Harold Pinter, *The Birthday Party*, 1958; London: Faber
Arnold Wesker, *Roots*, 1959: London: Methuen Drama

Background to *A Taste of Honey*

Kenneth Allsop, *The Angry Decade*, London: Peter Owen, 1958
Howard Goorney, *The Theatre Workshop Story*, London: Methuen, 1981
Laurence Kitchin, *Mid-Century Drama*, London: Faber, revised 1962
Lacey, Stephen, *British Realist Theatre: The New Wave in its Context 1956–1965*, London: Routledge, 1995
Peter Lewis, *The Fifties*, London: Heinemann, 1978
Charles Marowitz, Tom Milne, Owen Hale (eds), *New Theatre Voices of the Fifties and Sixties – Selections from Encore Magazine 1956–63*, London: Methuen, 1981
Charles Marowitz and Simon Trussler (eds), *Theatre at Work*, London: Methuen, 1967
Rebellato, Dan, *1956 and All That: The Making of Modern British Drama*, London: Routledge, 1999
John Russell Taylor, *Anger and After*, London: Methuen, revised 1969

Feminist Critical Responses to *A Taste of Honey*

Bennett, Susan, 'New Plays and Women's Voices in the 1950s', in Elaine Aston and Janelle Reinelt (eds), *Modern British Women Playwrights*, Cambridge: Cambridge University Press, 2000, pp. 38–52
Case, Sue-Ellen, 'The Power of Sex: English Plays by Women, 1958–1988, *New Theatre Quarterly*, August 1991, pp. 238–45

Keyssar, Helene, 'Foothills: Precursors of Feminist Drama', in
    Feminist Theatre, Basingstoke: Macmillan, 1984
Taylor, Lib, 'Early Stages: Women Dramatists 1958–68' in Trevor
    R. Griffiths and Margaret Llewellyn-Jones, *British and Irish
    Women Dramatists Since 1958*, Buckingham: Open University
    Press, 1993, pp. 9–25
Wandor, Michelene, 'The 1950s' in *Post-War British Drama:
    Looking Back in Gender*, London: Routledge, 2001, pp. 41–75

Jo, with Helen (*above*) and with Peter (*below*). From the film (1962)

Joe with Boyfriend (*above*). Helen with Peter (*below*). Both from the 1962 film.

Peter and Helen in the pub (*above*). Jo and Geof (*below*). Both from the 1962 film.

Jo and Geof. From the 1962 film.

A Taste of Honey

This play was first presented by Theatre Workshop at the Theatre Royal, Stratford, London E15, on 27 May 1958.

On 10 February 1959 the play was presented by Donald Albery and Oscar Lewenstein Ltd, at Wyndham's Theatre, London, with the following cast:

HELEN	Avis Bunnage
JOSEPHINE, *her daughter*	Frances Cuka
PETER, *her friend*	Nigel Davenport
THE BOY	Clifton Jones
GEOFFREY	Murray Melvin
THE APEX JAZZ TRIO	Johnny Wallbank (*cornet*)
	Barry Wright (*guitar*)
	Christopher Capon (*double bass*)
SETTING BY	John Bury
COSTUMES BY	Una Collins

The play is set in Salford, Lancashire, today

Directed by Joan Littlewood

Act One

SCENE ONE

The stage represents a comfortless flat in Manchester and the street outside. Jazz music. Enter HELEN, *a semi-whore, and her daughter,* JO. *They are loaded with baggage.*

HELEN: Well! This is the place.

JO: And I don't like it.

HELEN: When I find somewhere for us to live I have to consider something far more important than your feelings . . . the rent. It's all I can afford.

JO: You can afford something better than this old ruin.

HELEN: When you start earning you can start moaning.

JO: Can't be soon enough for me. I'm cold and my shoes let water . . . what a place . . . and we're supposed to be living off her immoral earnings.

HELEN: I'm careful. Anyway, what's wrong with this place? Everything in it's falling apart, it's true, and we've no heating – but there's a lovely view of the gasworks, we share a bathroom with the community and this wallpaper's contemporary. What more do you want? Anyway it'll do for us. Pass me a glass, Jo.

JO: Where are they?

HELEN: I don't know.

JO: You packed 'em. She'd lose her head if it was loose.

HELEN: Here they are. I put 'em in my bag for safety. Pass me that bottle – it's in the carrier.

JO: Why should I run round after you? [*Takes whisky bottle from bag.*]

HELEN: Children owe their parents these little attentions.

JO: I don't owe you a thing.

HELEN: Except respect, and I don't seem to get any of that.

JO: Drink, drink, drink, that's all you're fit for. You make me sick.

HELEN: Others may pray for their daily bread, I pray for . . .

JO: Is that the bedroom?

HELEN: It is. Your health, Jo.

JO: We're sharing a bed again, I see.

HELEN: Of course, you know I can't bear to be parted from you.

JO: What I wouldn't give for a room of my own! God! It's freezing! Isn't there any sort of fire anywhere, Helen?

HELEN: Yes, there's a gas-propelled thing somewhere.

JO: Where?

HELEN: Where? What were you given eyes for? Do you want me to carry you about? Don't stand there shivering; have some of this if you're so cold.

JO: You know I don't like it.

HELEN: Have you tried it?

JO: No.

HELEN: Then get it down you! [*She wanders around the room searching for fire.*] "Where!" she says. She can never see anything till she falls over it. Now, where's it got to? I know I saw it here somewhere . . . one of those shilling in the slot affairs; the landlady pointed it out to me as part of the furniture and fittings. I don't know. Oh! It'll turn up. What's up with you now?

JO: I don't like the smell of it.

HELEN: You don't smell it, you drink it! It consoles you.

JO: What do you need consoling about?

HELEN: Life! Come on, give it to me if you've done with it. I'll soon put it in a safe place. [*Drinks.*]

JO: You're knocking it back worse than ever.

HELEN: Oh! Well, it's one way of passing time while I'm

waiting for something to turn up. And it usually does if I drink hard enough. Oh my God! I've caught a shocking cold from somebody. Have you got a clean hanky, Jo? Mine's wringing wet with dabbing at my nose all day.

JO: Have this, it's nearly clean. Isn't that light awful? I do hate to see an unshaded electric light bulb dangling from the ceiling like that.

HELEN: Well, don't look at it then.

JO: Can I have that chair, Helen? I'll put my scarf round it. [JO *takes chair from* HELEN, *stands on it and wraps her scarf round light bulb – burning herself in the process.*]

HELEN: Wouldn't she get on your nerves? Just when I was going to take the weight off my feet for five minutes. Oh! my poor old nose.

JO: Christ! It's hot.

HELEN: Why can't you leave things alone? Oh! she gets me down. I'll buy a proper shade tomorrow. It's running like a tap. This is the third hanky today.

JO: Tomorrow? What makes you think we're going to live that long? The roof's leaking!

HELEN: Is it? No, it's not, it's just condensation.

JO: Was it raining when you took the place?

HELEN: It is a bit of a mess, isn't it.

JO: You always have to rush off into things. You never think.

HELEN: Oh well, we can always find something else.

JO: But what are you looking for? Every place we find is the same.

HELEN: Oh! Every time I turn my head my eyeballs hurt. Can't we have a bit of peace for five minutes?

JO: I'll make some coffee.

HELEN: Do what you like. I feel rotten. I've no business being out of bed.

JO: Where's the kitchen?

HELEN: Where's the – through there. I have to be really bad before I can go to bed, though. It's the only redeeming feature in this entire lodging house. I've got it in my throat now too. I hope you're going to make full use of it.

JO: There's a gas stove in here.

HELEN: It hurts when I swallow. Of course there is!

JO: It looks a bit ancient. How do I light it?

HELEN: How do I – with a match. Wouldn't she drive you mad?

JO: I know that, but which knob do I turn?

HELEN: Turn 'em all, you're bound to find the right one in the end. She can't do a thing for herself, that girl. Mind you don't gas yourself. Every time I comb my hair it goes right through me. I think it's more than a cold, you know – more likely it's 'flu! Did you find it?
[*Loud bang.*]

JO: Yes.

HELEN: The way she bangs about! I tell you, my head's coming off.

JO: Won't be long now. Who lives here besides us, Helen? Any young people?

HELEN: Eh? Oh! Yes, I did see a lad hanging around here when I called last week. Handsome, long-legged creature – just the way I like 'em. Perhaps he's one of the fixtures. He'd just do for you, Jo; you've never had a boy friend, have you?

JO: No. I used to like one of your fancy men though.

HELEN: Oh! Which one?

JO: I thought I was in love with him.

HELEN: Which one does she mean?

JO: I thought he was the only man I'd ever love in my life and then he ran off with that landlady's daughter.

HELEN: Oh! Him.

JO: And I cried myself to sleep for weeks.

HELEN: She was a silly cat if ever there was one. You should have seen her. Honest to God! She was a sight for sore eyes. I'll have to tell you about her too sometime.

JO: I saw him again one day, on the street.

HELEN: Did you?

JO: I couldn't believe my eyes. He was thin, weak-chinned, with a funny turned-up nose.

HELEN: It wasn't his nose I was interested in.

[*Tugboat heard.*]

JO: Can you smell that river?

HELEN: I can't smell a thing! I've got such a cold.

JO: What's that big place over there?

HELEN: The slaughterhouse. Where all the cows, sheep and pigs go in and all the beef, pork and mutton comes out.

JO: I wonder what it'll be like here in the summer. I bet it'll smell.

HELEN: This whole city smells. Eee, there's a terrible draught in here. Where's it coming from? Look at that! What a damn silly place to put a window. This place is cold enough, isn't it, without giving shelter to the four winds.

JO: Helen, stop sniffing. It sounds awful.

HELEN: I can't help it. You'd sniff if you had a cold like this. She's not got a bit of consideration in her. It's self all the time.

JO: I'm going to unpack my bulbs. I wonder where I can put them.

HELEN: I could tell you.

JO: They're supposed to be left in a cool, dark place.

HELEN: That's where we all end up sooner or later. Still, it's no use worrying, is it?

JO: I hope they bloom. Always before when I've tried to fix up a window box nothin's ever grown in it.

HELEN: Why do you bother?

JO: It's nice to see a few flowers, isn't it?

HELEN: Where did you get those bulbs?

JO: The Park. The gardener had just planted about two hundred. I didn't think he'd miss half a dozen.

HELEN: That's the way to do things. If you see something

you want, take it. That's my daughter for you. If you spent half as much time on me as you do on them fiddling bits of greenery I'd be a damn sight better off. Go and see if that kettle's boiling.

JO: See yourself. I've got to find somewhere for my bulbs.

HELEN: See yourself! Do everything yourself. That's what happens. You bring 'em up and they turn round and talk to you like that. I would never have dared talk to my mother like that when I was her age. She'd have knocked me into the middle of next week. Oh! my head. Whenever I walk, you know how it is! What a journey! I never realized this city was so big. Have we got any aspirins left, Jo?

JO: No. I dreamt about you last night, Helen.

HELEN: You're going to have a shocking journey to school each day, aren't you? It must be miles and miles.

JO: Not for much longer.

HELEN: Why, are you still set on leaving school at Christmas?

JO: Yes.

HELEN: What are you going to do?

JO: Get out of your sight as soon as I can get a bit of money in my pocket.

HELEN: Very wise too. But how are you going to get your money in the first place? After all, you're not very fond of work, are you?

JO: No. I take after you.

HELEN [*looking at the aspidistra*]: That's nice, isn't it? Puts me in mind of my first job, in a tatty little pub down Whit Lane. I thought it was wonderful ... You know, playing the piano and all that; a real get-together at weekends. Everybody standing up and giving a song. I used to bring the house down with this one. [*Sings.*]

> I'd give the song birds to the wild wood
> I'd give the sunset to the blind

And to the old folks I'd give the memory
of the baby upon their knee.

[*To orchestra*]: Come on, vamp it in with me.

JO: You can't play to that. It's got no rhythm.

HELEN: Oh! They'd tear it up, wouldn't they? [*She sings another verse.*] It's nice though isn't it?

JO: What would you say if I did something like that?

HELEN: I should have taken up singing – everybody used to tell me. What did you say?

JO: I said what would you say if I got a job in a pub?

HELEN: You can't sing, can you? Anyway, it's your life, ruin it your own way. It's a waste of time interfering with other people, don't you think so? It takes me all my time to look after myself, I know that.

JO: That's what you said, but really you think you could make a better job of it, don't you?

HELEN: What?

JO: Ruining my life. After all, you've had plenty of practice.

HELEN: Yes, give praise where praise is due, I always say. I certainly supervised my own downfall. Oh! This chair's a bit low, isn't it? Could do with a cushion.

JO: Anyway I'm not getting married like you did.

HELEN: Oh!

JO: I'm too young and beautiful for that.

HELEN: Listen to it! Still, we all have funny ideas at that age, don't we – makes no difference though, we all end up same way sooner or later. Anyway, tell me about this dream you had.

JO: What dream?

HELEN: You said you had a dream about me.

JO: Oh that! It was nothing much. I was standing in a garden and there were some policemen digging and guess what they found planted under a rosebush?

HELEN: You.

JO: No – you.

HELEN: Why, had we run short of cemetery space? Well, I've always said we should be used for manure when we're gone. Go and see to that coffee. I'm dying for a hot drink. This bloody cold! It's all over me. I'm sure it's 'flu – I suppose I'd better clear some of this stuff away. She wouldn't think. Well, they don't at that age, do they? Oh! It gets me right here when I try to do anything when I bend, you know. Have you ever had it? I was thinking of washing my hair tonight, but I don't think it's wise to . . . Christ! what the hell's she got in here . . . sooner her than me . . . what's this? [*Seeing drawings.*] Hey, Jo, Jo, what's this?

JO: What's what?

HELEN: Did you do this?

JO: Put it down.

HELEN: I thought you said you weren't good at anything.

JO: It's only a drawing.

HELEN: It's very good. Did you show them this at school?

JO: I'm never at one school long enough to show them anything.

HELEN: That's my fault, I suppose.

JO: You will wander about the country.

HELEN: It's the gipsy in me. I didn't realize I had such a talented daughter. Look at that. It's good, isn't it?

JO: I'm not just talented, I'm geniused.

HELEN: I think I'll hang this on the wall somewhere. Now, where will it be least noticeable? Don't snatch. Have you no manners? What's these?

JO: Self-portraits. Give 'em here.

HELEN: Self-portraits? Oh! Well, I suppose you've got to draw pictures of yourself, nobody else would. Hey! Is that supposed to be me?

JO: Yes.

HELEN: Don't I look a misery? They're very artistic though,

I must say. Have you ever thought of going to a proper art school and getting a proper training?

JO: It's too late.

HELEN: I'll pay, You're not stupid. You'll soon learn.

JO: I've had enough of school. Too many different schools and too many different places.

HELEN: You're wasting yourself.

JO: So long as I don't waste anybody else. Why are you so suddenly interested in me, anyway? You've never cared much before about what I was doing or what I was trying to do or the difference between them.

HELEN: I know, I'm a cruel, wicked woman.

JO: Why did we have to come here anyway? We were all right at the other place.

HELEN: I was fed up with the other place.

JO: You mean you're running away from somebody.

HELEN: You're asking for a bloody good hiding, lady. Just be careful. Oh! She'd drive you out of your mind. And my head's splitting. Splitting in two.

JO: What about me? Don't you think I get fed up with all this flitting about? Where's the bathroom? I'm going to have a bath.

HELEN: You're always bathing.

JO: I'm not like you. I don't wait until it becomes necessary before I have a good wash.

HELEN: You'll find the communal latrine and wash-house at the end of the passage. And don't throw your things about, this place is untidy enough as it is.

JO: That's all we do, live out of a travelling-bag.

HELEN: Don't worry, you'll soon be an independent working woman and free to go where you please.

JO: The sooner the better. I'm sick of you. You've made my life a misery. And stop sneezing your 'flu bugs all over me. I don't want to catch your cold.

HELEN: Oh! Get out of my sight. Go and have your bath.

JO: You can get your own coffee too. Why should I do anything for you? You never do anything for me.

[*Music. Enter* PETER, *a brash car salesman, cigar in mouth.*]

HELEN: Oh! My God! Look what the wind's blown in. What do you want?

PETER: Just passing by, you know. Thought I'd take a look at your new headquarters.

HELEN: Just passing ... How did you find my address?

PETER: I found it. Did you think you could escape me, dear?

JO: So that's what she was running away from.

PETER: Who's this?

HELEN: My daughter.

PETER: Oh! Hello there. That puts another ten years on her.

JO: What's this one called?

HELEN: Smith.

JO: You told me not to trust men calling themselves Smith.

HELEN: Oh go and have your bath.

JO: I don't know where the bathroom is.

HELEN: It's in a little hole in the corridor.

JO: Is he staying?

PETER: Yes, I'm staying.

JO: Then I'll go for my bath later.

HELEN: What did you want to follow me here for?

PETER [*fumbling*]: You know what I want.

HELEN: Give over! Jo, go and see to that coffee! He would show up just when I've got her hanging round my neck.

PETER: Do what your mother tells you.

JO: Ordering me about like a servant! [*She goes.* PETER *makes another pass at* HELEN.] The kettle's not boiling. I suppose she hasn't told you about me.

PETER: Christ!

HELEN: Go and lay the table.

JO: No.

HELEN: Well, do something. Turn yourself into a bloody

termite and crawl into the wall or something, but make yourself scarce.

PETER: Get rid of her.

HELEN: I can't. Anyway, nobody asked you to come here.

PETER: Why did you come here? I had to chase all over town looking for you, only to finish up in this dump.

HELEN: Oh shut up! I've got a cold.

PETER: What on earth made you choose such a ghastly district?

HELEN: I can't afford to be so classy.

PETER: Tenements, cemetery, slaughterhouse.

HELEN: Oh we've got the lot here.

PETER: Nobody could live in a place like this.

JO: Only about fifty thousand people.

PETER: And a snotty-nosed daughter.

HELEN: I said nobody asked you to come. Oh my God! I'll have to have a dose of something. My head's swimming. Why did you?

PETER: Why did I what?

HELEN: Follow me here?

PETER: Now you know you're glad to see me, kid.

HELEN: No I'm not. The only consolation I can find in your immediate presence is your ultimate absence.

PETER: In that case, I'll stay.

HELEN: I warned you. I told you I was throwing my hand in. Now didn't I?

PETER: You did.

HELEN: Oh! Throw that cigar away. It looks bloody ridiculous stuck in your mouth like a horizontal chimney.

PETER: Your nose is damp. Here, have this.

HELEN: Oh go away!

PETER: Give it a good blow.

HELEN: Leave it alone.

PETER: Blow your nose, woman. [*She does*]. And while you're at it blow a few of those cobwebs out of your head. You can't afford to lose a man like me.

HELEN: Can't I?

PETER: This is the old firm. You can't renege on the old firm.

HELEN: I'm a free lance. Besides, I'm thinking of giving it up.

PETER: What?

HELEN: Sex! Men!

PETER: What have we done to deserve this?

HELEN: It's not what you've done. It's what I've done.

PETER: But [*approaching her*], darling, you do it so well.

HELEN: Now give over, Peter. I've got all these things to unpack.

PETER: Send her to the pictures.

HELEN: I don't feel like it.

PETER: What's wrong?

HELEN: I'm tired. It's terrible when you've got a cold, isn't it? You don't fancy anything.

PETER: Well, put your hat on, let's go for a drink. Come on down to the church and I'll make an honest woman of you.

HELEN [*she goes to put her coat on, then changes her mind*]: No, I don't fancy it.

PETER: I'm offering to marry you, dear.

HELEN: You what?

PETER: Come on, let's go for a drink.

HELEN: I told you I don't fancy it.

PETER: You won't find anything better.

HELEN: Listen, love, I'm old enough to be your mother.

PETER [*petting her*]: Now you know I like this mother and son relationship.

HELEN: Stop it!

PETER: Aren't you wearing your girdle?

HELEN: Now, Peter.

PETER: Whoops!

HELEN: Well, you certainly liberate something in me. And I don't think it's maternal instincts either.

PETER [*sings*]: "Walter, Walter, lead me to the altar!"

HELEN: Some hopes.

PETER: Helen, you don't seem to realize what an opportunity I'm giving you. The world is littered with women I've rejected, women still anxious to indulge my little vices and excuse my less seemly virtues. Marry me, Helen. I'm young, good-looking and well set up. I may never ask you again.

HELEN: You're drunk.

PETER: I'm as sober as a judge.

HELEN: If you ask me again I might accept.

PETER [*sings*]: "I see a quiet place, a fireplace, a cosy room."

HELEN: Yes, the tap room at the Red Lion. What are you after?

PETER: You know what I like.

JO [*coughs, enters*]: Here's your coffee. Excuse me if I interrupted something. I'm sorry the crockery isn't very elegant, but it's all we've got.

PETER: Don't run away.

JO: I'm not running. [*Sits.*]

PETER: Is she always like this?

HELEN: She's jealous . . .

PETER: That's something I didn't bargain for.

HELEN: Can't bear to see me being affectionate with anybody.

JO: You've certainly never been affectionate with me.

PETER: Still, she's old enough to take care of herself. What sort of coffee is this anyway? It can hardly squeeze itself through the spout.

HELEN: She always does that. Makes it as weak as she can because she knows I like it strong. Don't drink that, it isn't worth drinking. Leave it.

JO: She should be in bed.

PETER: I know she should.

JO: You look very pale and sickly, Helen.

HELEN: Thank you.

JO: Is he going?

HELEN: Yes, come on, you'd better go before you catch my cold.

[*He pulls her to him as she passes.*]

PETER: Come outside then.

HELEN: No.

PETER: What does the little lady want? An engagement ring?

JO: I should have thought their courtship had passed the stage of symbolism.

HELEN: I always accept the odd diamond ring with pleasure.

PETER: I know it's my money you're after.

HELEN: Are you kidding?

JO: Hey!

[*He embraces* HELEN *at the door and begins to tell her a dirty story.*]

PETER: Did I ever tell you about the bookie who married the prostitute?

HELEN: No. Go on.

JO: Hey! What sort of a cigar is that?

PETER: Why don't you go home to your father?

JO: He's dead.

PETER: Too bad. Anyway, this bookie . . .

JO: Is it a Havana?

HELEN: Yes.

PETER: A rich, dark Havana, rolled on the thigh of a coal black mammy.

JO: You want to be careful. You never know where a coal black mammy's thigh's been.

HELEN: Take no notice of her. She think's she's funny.

JO: So does he! I bet he's married.

[HELEN *bursts out laughing at his joke.*]

You're not really going to marry her, are you? She's a devil with the men.

PETER: Are you Helen?

HELEN: Well, I don't consider myself a slouch. Now come on then, if you've finished what you came for you'd better get going. We've all this to clear away before we go to bed.

PETER: Well, I won't be round tomorrow; the cat's been on the strawberries.

HELEN: Get going.

PETER: Don't forget me.

JO: Shall I withdraw while you kiss her good night?

HELEN: I'll kiss you good night in a minute, lady, and it really will be good night.

PETER: Well, take care of your mother while she's ailing, Jo. You know how fragile these old ladies are.

HELEN: Go on, get! [*Exit* PETER.] Well, I'm going to bed. We'll shift this lot tomorrow. There's always another day.

JO: It's dark out there now. I think I'll have my bath in the morning.

HELEN: Are you afraid of the dark?

JO: You know I am.

HELEN: You should try not to be.

JO: I do.

HELEN: And you're still afraid?

JO: Yes.

HELEN: Then you'll have to try a bit harder, won't you?

JO: Thanks. I'll do that. What's the bed like?

HELEN: Like a coffin only not half as comfortable.

JO: Have you ever tried a coffin?

HELEN: I dare say I will one day. I do wish we had a hot water bottle.

JO: You should have asked him to stay. It wouldn't be the first time I've been thrown out of my bed to make room for one of your . . .

HELEN: For God's sake shut up! Close your mouth for five minutes. And you can turn the light off and come to bed.

JO: Aren't we going to clear this lot up?

HELEN: No, it'll look all right in the dark.

JO: Yes, it's seen at its best, this room, in the dark.

HELEN: Everything is seen at its best in the dark – including me. I love it. Can't understand why you're so scared of it.

JO: I'm not frightened of the darkness outside. It's the darkness inside houses I don't like.

HELEN: Come on! Hey, Jo, what would you do if I told you I was thinking of getting married again?

JO: I'd have you locked up in an institution right away!

HELEN: Come on.

[*Music. Fade out.*]

SCENE TWO

JO *and her* BOY FRIEND, *a coloured naval rating, walking on the street. They stop by the door.*

JO: I'd better go in now. Thanks for carrying my books.

BOY: Were you surprised to see me waiting outside school?

JO: Not really.

BOY: Glad I came?

JO: You know I am.

BOY: So am I.

JO: Well, I'd better go in.

BOY: Not yet! Stay a bit longer.

JO: All right! Doesn't it go dark early? I like winter. I like it better than all the other seasons.

BOY: I like it too. When it goes dark early it gives me more time for – [*He kisses her.*]

JO: Don't do that. You're always doing it.

BOY: You like it.

JO: I know, but I don't want to do it all the time.

BOY: Afraid someone'll see us?

JO: I don't care.

BOY: Say that again.

JO: I don't care.

BOY: You mean it too. You're the first girl I've met who really didn't care. Listen, I'm going to ask you something. I'm a man of few words. Will you marry me?

JO: Well, I'm a girl of few words. I won't marry you but you've talked me into it.

BOY: How old are you?

JO: Nearly eighteen.

BOY: And you really will marry me?

JO: I said so, didn't I? You shouldn't have asked me if you were only kidding me up. [*She starts to go.*]

BOY: Hey! I wasn't kidding. I thought you were. Do you really mean it? You will marry me?

JO: I love you.

BOY: How do you know?

JO: I don't know why I love you but I do.

BOY: I adore you. [*Swinging her through the air.*]

JO: So do I. I can't resist myself.

BOY: I've got something for you.

JO: What is it? A ring!

BOY: This morning in the shop I couldn't remember what sort of hands you had, long hands, small hands or what. I stood there like a damn fool trying to remember what they felt like. [*He puts the ring on and kisses her hand.*] What will your mother say?

JO: She'll probably laugh.

BOY: Doesn't she care who her daughter marries?

JO: She's not marrying you, I am. It's got nothing to do with her.

BOY: She hasn't seen me.

JO: And when she does?

BOY: She'll see a coloured boy.

JO: No, whatever else she might be, she isn't prejudiced against colour. You're not worried about it, are you?

BOY: So long as you like it.

JO: You know I do.

BOY: Well, that's all that matters.

JO: When shall we get married?

BOY: My next leave? It's a long time, six months.

JO: It'll give us a chance to save a bit of money. Here, see . . . this ring . . . it's too big; look, it slides about . . . And I couldn't wear it for school anyway. I might lose it. Let's go all romantic. Have you got a bit of string?

BOY: What for?

JO: I'm going to tie it round my neck. Come on, turn your pockets out. Three handkerchiefs, a safety pin, a screw! Did that drop out of your head? Elastic bands! Don't little boys carry some trash. And what's this?

BOY: Nothing.

JO: A toy car! Does it go?

BOY: Hm hm!

JO: Can I try it? [*She does.*]

BOY: She doesn't even know how it works. Look, not like that.

[*He makes it go fast.*]

JO: I like that. Can I keep it?

BOY: Yes, take it, my soul and all, everything.

JO: Thanks. I know, I can use my hair ribbon for my ring. Do it up for me.

BOY: Pretty neck you've got.

JO: Glad you like it. It's my schoolgirl complexion. I'd better tuck this out of sight. I don't want my mother to see it. She'd only laugh. Did I tell you, when I leave school this week I start a part-time job in a bar? Then as soon as I get a full-time job, I'm leaving Helen and starting up in a room somewhere.

BOY: I wish I wasn't in the Navy.

JO: Why?

BOY: We won't have much time together.

JO: Well, we can't be together all the time and all the time there is wouldn't be enough.

BOY: It's a sad story, Jo. Once, I was a happy young man, not a care in the world. Now! I'm trapped into a barbaric cult . . .

JO: What's that? Mau-Mau?

BOY: Matrimony.

JO: Trapped! I like that! You almost begged me to marry you.

BOY: You led me on. I'm a trusting soul. Who took me down to that deserted football pitch?

JO: Who found the football pitch? I didn't even know it existed. And it just shows how often you must have been there, too . . . you certainly know where all the best spots are. I'm not going there again . . . It's too quiet. Anything might happen to a girl.

BOY: It almost did. You shameless woman!

JO: That's you taking advantage of my innocence.

BOY: I didn't take advantage. I had scruples.

JO: You would have done. You'd have gone as far as I would have let you and no scruples would have stood in your way.

BOY: You enjoyed it as much as I did.

JO: Shut up! This is the sort of conversation that can colour a young girl's mind.

BOY: Women never have young minds. They are born three thousand years old.

JO: Sometimes you look three thousand years old. Did your ancestors come from Africa?

BOY: No. Cardiff. Disappointed? Were you hoping to marry a man whose father beat the tom-tom all night?

JO: I don't care where you were born. There's still a bit of jungle in you somewhere. [*A siren is heard*]. I'm going in now, I'm hungry. A young girl's got to eat, you know.

BOY: Honey, you've got to stop eating. No more food, no more make-up, no more fancy clothes; we're saving up to get married.

JO: I just need some new clothes too. I've only got this one coat. I have to use it for school and when I go out with you. I do feel a mess.

BOY: You look all right to me.

JO: Shall I see you tonight?

BOY: No, I got work to do.

JO: What sort of work?

BOY: Hard work, it involves a lot of walking.

JO: And a lot of walking makes you thirsty. I know, you're going drinking.

BOY: That's right. It's one of the lads' birthdays. I'll see you tomorrow.

JO: All right. I'll tell you what, I won't bother going to school and we can spend the whole day together. I'll meet you down by that ladies' hairdressing place.

BOY: The place that smells of cooking hair?

JO: Yes, about ten o'clock.

BOY: Okay, you're the boss.

JO: Good night.

BOY: Aren't you going to kiss me good night?

JO: You know I am. [*Kisses him.*] I like kissing you. Good night.

BOY: Good night.

JO: Dream of me.

BOY: I dreamt about you last night. Fell out of bed twice.

JO: You're in a bad way.

BOY: You bet I am. Be seeing you!

JO [*as she goes*]: I love you.

BOY: Why?

JO: Because you're daft.

[*He waves good-bye, turns and sings to the audience, and goes. HELEN dances on to the music, lies down and reads an evening paper. JO dances on dreamily.*]

HELEN: You're a bit late coming home from school, aren't you?

JO: I met a friend.

HELEN: Well, he certainly knows how to put stars in your eyes.

JO: What makes you think it's a he?

HELEN: Well, I certainly hope it isn't a she who makes you walk round in this state.

JO: He's a sailor.

HELEN: I hope you exercised proper control over his nautical ardour. I've met a few sailors myself.

JO: He's lovely.

HELEN: Is he?

JO: He's got beautiful brown eyes and gorgeous curly hair.

HELEN: Has he got long legs?

JO: They're all right.

HELEN: How old is he?

JO: Twenty-two. He's doing his national service, but before that he was a male nurse.

HELEN: A male nurse, eh? That's interesting. Where did he do his nursing?

JO: In a hospital, of course! Where else do they have nurses?

HELEN: Does he ever get any free samples? We could do with a few contacts for things like that.

JO: Oh shut up, Helen. Have a look in that paper and see what's on at the pictures tomorrow night.

HELEN: Where is it? Oh yes ... *I was a Teenage* ... what? You can't go there anyway, it's a proper little flea pit. *The Ten Commandments*, here that'd do you good. *Desire Under the* ... oh! What a funny place to have desire! You might as well have it at home as anywhere else, mightn't you? No, there's nothing here that I fancy.

JO: You never go to the pictures.

HELEN: I used to but the cinema has become more and more like the theatre, it's all mauling and muttering, can't hear what they're saying half the time and when you do it's not worth listening to. Look at that advertisement. It's porno-graphic. In my opinion such a frank and open display of the female form can only induce little boys of all ages to add vulgar comments in pencil. I ask you, what sort of an inflated woman is that? She's got bosom, bosom and still more bosom. I bet every inch of her chest is worth it's weight in gold. Let's have a look at you. I wonder if I could turn you into a mountain of voluptuous temptation?

JO: Why?

HELEN: I'd put you on films.

JO: I'd sooner be put on't streets. It's more honest.

HELEN: You might have to do that yet.

JO: Where did this magazine come from?

HELEN: Woman downstairs give it me.

JO: I didn't think you'd buy it.

HELEN: Why buy when it's cheaper to borrow?

JO: What day was I born on?

HELEN: I don't know.

JO: You should remember such an important event.

HELEN: I've always done my best to forget that.

JO: How old was I when your husband threw you out?

HELEN: Change the subject. When I think of her father and my husband it makes me wonder why I ever bothered, it does really.

JO: He was rich, wasn't he . . .

HELEN: He was a rat!

JO: He was your husband. Why did you marry him?

HELEN: At the time I had nothing better to do. Then he divorced me; that was your fault.

JO: I agree with him. If I was a man and my wife had a baby that wasn't mine I'd sling her out.

HELEN: Would you? It's a funny thing but I don't think I would. Still, why worry?

JO [reading from magazine]: It says here that Sheik Ahmed – an Arabian mystic – will, free of all charge, draw up for you a complete analysis of your character and destiny.

HELEN: Let's have a look.

JO: There's his photograph.

HELEN: Oh! He looks like a dirty little spiv. Listen Jo, don't bother your head about Arabian mystics. There's two w's in your future. Work or want, and no Arabian Knight can tell you different. We're all at the steering wheel of our own destiny. Careering along like drunken drivers. I'm going to get married. [*The news is received in silence.*] I said, I'm going to get married.

JO: Yes, I heard you the first time. What do you want me to do, laugh and throw pennies? Is it that Peter Smith?

HELEN: He's the unlucky man.

JO: You're centuries older than him.

HELEN: Only ten years.

JO: What use can a woman of that age be to anybody?

HELEN: I wish you wouldn't talk about me as if I'm an impotent, shrivelled old woman without a clue left in her head.

JO: You're not exactly a child bride.

HELEN: I have been one once, or near enough.

JO: Just imagine it, you're forty years old. I hope to be dead and buried before I reach that age. You've been living for forty years.

HELEN: Yes, it must be a biological phenomena.

JO: You don't look forty. You look a sort of well-preserved sixty.

[*Music. Enter* PETER *carrying a large bouquet and a box of chocolates and looking uncomfortable.*]

HELEN: Oh look, and it's all mine!

JO: Hello, Daddy.

PETER: Oh! So you told her.

HELEN: Of course. Come in and sit down. On second thoughts lie down, you look marvellous.

[*He gives her the bouquet.*]

Oh! really, you shouldn't have bothered yourself. I know

the thought was there, but ... here, Jo, have we got a
vase, put these in some water.

JO: How did she talk you into it? You must be out of your
mind.

PETER: That's possible, I suppose.

JO: Flowers and all the trimmings. Helen can't eat anything
sweet and delicious. She's got to watch her figure.

HELEN: Nonsense! My figure hasn't altered since I was
eighteen.

JO: Really?

HELEN: Not an inch.

JO: I hope I'm luckier with mine.

HELEN: Do you see anything objectionable about my figure,
Peter?

PETER: I find the whole thing most agreeable.

JO: You've got to say that, you're marrying it!

PETER: The chocolates are for you, Jo.

JO: Buying my silence, hey! It's a good idea. I like chocolates.

HELEN: Help yourself to a drink, Peter, and I'll go and put my
glad rags on. [*Exit.*]

PETER: Don't let's be long, huh? I've booked a table. Dammit,
I thought you'd be ready.

JO: She's got no sense of time.

PETER: Don't sit there guzzling all those chocolates at once.
[*She throws the lid at him.*]
What the hell are you playing at ... sit down and behave
yourself, you little snip.

JO: Hey! Don't start bossing me about. You're not my father.

PETER. Christ Almighty! Will you sit down and eat your
chocolates. Do what you like but leave me alone.
[*Suddenly she attacks him, half-laughing, half-crying.*]

JO: You leave me alone. And leave my mother alone too.
[HELEN *enters.*]

PETER: Get away! For God's sake go and ...

HELEN: Leave him alone, Jo. He doesn't want to be bothered

with you. Got a cigarette, Peter? Did you get yourself a
drink?

PETER: No, I ...

JO: Do I bother you, Mister Smith, or must I wait till we're
alone for an answer?

PETER: Can't you keep her under control?

HELEN: I'll knock her head round if she isn't careful. Be quiet,
Jo. And don't tease him.

PETER: Tonight's supposed to be a celebration.

JO: What of?

HELEN: He's found a house. Isn't he marvellous? Show her
the photo of it, Peter. I shan't be a tick!

JO: You've certainly fixed everything up behind my back.

HELEN: Don't you think it's nice? One of his pals had to sell,
moving into something smaller. [*Goes*].

[PETER *throws snap on to the table*.]

JO: It's not bad. White walls, tennis courts. Has it got a
swimming pool?

PETER: It has twelve swimming pools.

JO: Can I see the other photos?

PETER: Which photos?

JO: In your wallet. I suppose you thought I didn't notice.

PETER: Oh! These. Yes, well, that's a photograph of my
family, my mother, my father, my sister, my brother and
... [*To himself*.] all the rest of the little bastards.

JO: Is this a wedding group?

PETER: My brother's wedding.

JO: They only just made it, too, from the look of his wife. You
can tell she's going to have a baby.

PETER: Oh? Thank you.

JO: You can have it back if I can see the others.

PETER: Which others? What are you talking about?

JO: Do you want me to tell my mother?

PETER: I don't give a damn what you tell your mother.

JO: They're all women, aren't they? I bet you've had thousands of girl friends. What was this one with the long legs called?

PETER: Ah! Yes, number thirty-eight. A charming little thing.

JO: Why do you wear that black patch?

PETER: I lost an eye.

JO: Where?

PETER: During the war.

JO: Were you in the Navy?

PETER: Army.

JO: Officer?

PETER: Private.

JO: I thought you would have been somebody very important.

PETER: A private is far more important than you think. After all, who does all the dirty work?

JO: Yes, a general without any army wouldn't be much use, would he? Can I see your eye? I mean can I see the hole?

PETER: There's nothing to see.

JO: Do you wear that patch when you go to bed?

PETER: That's something about which I don't care to make a public statement.

JO: Tell me.

PETER: Well, there is one highly recommended way for a young girl to find out.

JO [*glancing through photos in wallet*]: I don't like this one. She's got too much stuff on her eyes.

PETER: That's the sort of thing your sex goes in for.

JO: I don't. I let my natural beauty shine through.

PETER: Is there no alternative?

JO: Don't you like shiny faces?

PETER: I suppose they're all right on sweet young things but I just don't go for sweet young things –

JO: Do you fancy me?

PETER: Not yet.

JO: You prefer old women.

PETER: She isn't old.

JO: She soon will be.

PETER: Ah well, that's love. [*Sings.*] "That wild, destructive thing called love."

JO: Why are you marrying Helen?

PETER: Why shouldn't I marry Helen?

JO: Your generation has some very peculiar ideas, that's all I can say.

PETER: Could I have my photographs back, please?

JO: There . . .

PETER: You don't like your mother much do you?

JO: She doesn't much care for me either.

PETER: I can understand that.

JO [*looking over his shoulder at photographs*]: I like that one with the shaggy hair cut. She's got nice legs too. Nearly as nice as mine.

PETER: Would you care for a smoke?

JO: Thanks.

[HELEN *is heard singing off stage*]:

HELEN: Jo! Where's my hat?

JO: I don't know. Where you left it. It's no use getting impatient, Peter. The art work takes a long time. Are you sure you lost your eye during the war? What happened?

PETER: Go and tell your mother I'll wait for her in the pub.

JO: Are you married?

PETER [*going*]: No, I'm still available.

HELEN [*entering*]: But only just.

PETER: Helen, you look utterly fantastic.

HELEN: Thanks. Put that cigarette out, Jo, you've got enough bad habits without adding to your repertoire. Do you like my hat, Peter?

PETER: Bang-on darling!

HELEN: What are all these books doing all over the place? Are you planning a moonlight flit, Jo? Stop it, Peter.

PETER: Got your blue garters on?

HELEN: Now, Peter. Come on, Jo, shift these books.

JO: I'm sorting them.

PETER [*taking* HELEN'S *hat*]: How do I look?

HELEN: Peter!

JO: Have you forgotten I'm leaving school this week?

HELEN: Peter, give it here. Stop fooling about. It took me ages to get this hat on right. Jo, do as you're told.

JO: All right.

HELEN: Peter! Don't do that. Give it to me. It's my best one. Put it down.

PETER [*to himself*]: No bloody sense of humour.

HELEN: What has she got there? Look at 'em. *Selected Nursery Rhymes,* Hans Andersen's *Fairy Tales, Pinocchio.* Well, you certainly go in for the more advanced types of literature. And what's this? The Holy Bible!

JO: You ought to read it. I think it's good.

HELEN: The extent of my credulity always depends on the extent of my alcoholic intake. Eat, drink and be merry –

JO: And live to regret it.

PETER: God! We've got a founder member of the Lord's Day Observance Society here.

JO: What are you marrying him for?

HELEN: He's got a wallet full of reasons.

JO: Yes. I've just seen 'em too.

HELEN: Can you give us a quid, Peter? I'd better leave her some money. We might decide to have a weekend at Blackpool and she can't live on grass and fresh air.

JO: I won't set eyes on her for a week now. I know her when she's in the mood. What are you going to do about me, Peter? The snotty-nosed daughter? Don't you think I'm a bit young to be left like this on my own while you flit off with my old woman?

PETER: She'll be all right, won't she? At her age.

HELEN: We can't take her with us. We will be, if you'll not take exception to the phrase, 'on our' honeymoon. Unless we change our minds.

PETER: I'm not having her with us.

HELEN: She can stay here then. Come on. I'm hungry.

JO: So am I.

HELEN: There's plenty of food in the kitchen.

JO: You should prepare my meals like a proper mother.

HELEN: Have I ever laid claim to being a proper mother? If you're too idle to cook your own meals you'll just have to cut food out of your diet altogether. That should help you lose a bit of weight, if nothing else.

PETER: She already looks like a bad case of malnutrition.

JO: Have you got your key, Helen? I might not be here when you decide to come back. I'm starting work on Saturday.

HELEN: Oh yes, she's been called to the bar.

PETER: What sort of a bar?

JO: The sort you're always propping up. I'm carrying on the family traditions. Will you give me some money for a new dress, Helen?

HELEN: If you really want to make a good investment, you'll buy a needle and some cotton. Every article of clothing on her back is held together by a safety pin or a knot. If she had an accident in the street I'd be ashamed to claim her.

PETER: Are we going?

JO: Can't I come with you?

HELEN: Shut up! You're going to have him upset. You jealous little cat! Come on, Peter.

PETER: All right, all right, don't pull. Don't get excited. And don't get impatient. Those bloody little street kids have probably pulled the car to pieces by now but we needn't worry about that, need we . . .

HELEN: I told you you'd upset him.

PETER: Upset? I'm not upset. I just want to get to hell out of this black hole of Calcutta.

[*They leave flat.* JO *looks after them for a moment then turns to bed – she lies across it, crying. Music.* BLACK BOY *enters.*]

BOY [*calling*]: Jo!

[*She doesn't move.*]

BOY: Joee!

JO: Coming.

[*They move towards each other as if dancing to the music. The music goes, the lights change.*]

JO: Oh! It's you! Come in. Just when I'm feeling and looking a mess.

BOY: What's wrong? You been crying?

JO: No.

BOY: You have. Your eyes are red.

JO: I don't cry. I've got a cold.

BOY: I think you have, too. Yes, you've got a bit of a temperature. Have you been eating?

JO: No.

BOY: You're a fine sight. Where's the kitchen?

JO: Through there. What are you going to do?

BOY: Fix you a cold cure. Where do you keep the milk?

JO: Under the sink. I hate milk.

BOY: I hate dirt. And this is just the dirtiest place I've ever seen. The children round here are filthy.

JO: It's their parents' fault. What are you putting in that milk?

BOY: A pill.

JO: I bet it's an opium pellet. I've heard about men like you.

BOY: There isn't another man like me anywhere. I'm one on his own.

JO: So am I.

BOY: Who was that fancy bit I saw stepping out of here a few minutes ago?

JO: If she was dressed up like Hope Gardens it was my mother.

BOY: And who is the Pirate King?

JO: She's marrying him. Poor devil!

BOY: You'll make a pretty bridesmaid.

JO: Bridesmaid! I'd sooner go to my own funeral.

BOY: You'd better drink this first.

JO: I don't like it.

BOY: Get it down you.

JO: But look, it's got skin on the top.

BOY: Don't whine. I'm not spending the evening with a running-nosed wreck. Finish your milk.

JO: Did you treat your patients in hospital like this?

BOY: Not unless they were difficult. Your mother looks very young, Jo, to have a daughter as old as you.

JO: She can still have children.

BOY: Well, that's an interesting bit of news. Why should I worry if she can have children or not?

JO: Do you fancy her?

BOY: That isn't the sort of question you ask your fiancé.

JO: It doesn't really matter if you do fancy her, anyway, because she's gone. You're too late. You've had your chips.

BOY: I'll be gone soon, too. What then?

JO: My heart's broke.

BOY: You can lie in bed at night and hear my ship passing down the old canal. It's cold in here. No fire?

JO: It doesn't work.

BOY: Come and sit down here. You can keep me warm.

JO: Is it warm where you're going?

BOY: I guess so.

JO: We could do with a bit of sunshine. In this country there are only two seasons, winter and winter. Do you think Helen's beautiful?

BOY: Who's Helen?

JO: My mother. Honestly, you are slow sometimes. Well, do you think she's beautiful.?

BOY: Yes.

JO: Am I like her?

BOY: No, you're not at all like her.

JO: Good. I'm glad nobody can see a resemblance between us.

BOY: My ring's still round your neck. Wear it. Your mother isn't here to laugh.

JO: Unfasten it, then.

BOY: Pretty neck you've got.

JO: Glad you like it.

BOY: No! Let me put it on.

JO: Did it cost very much?

BOY: You shouldn't ask questions like that. I got it from Woolworths!

JO: Woolworth's best! I don't care. I'm not proud. It's the thought that counts and I wonder what thought it was in your wicked mind that made you buy it.

BOY: I've got dishonourable intentions.

JO: I'm so glad.

BOY: Are you? [*He embraces her.*]

JO: Stop it.

BOY: Why? Do you object to the "gross clasps of the lascivious Moor"?

JO: Who said that?

BOY: Shakespeare in *Othello*.

JO: Oh! Him. He said everything, didn't he?

BOY: Let me be your Othello and you my Desdemona.

JO: All right.

BOY: "Oh ill-starred wench."

JO: Will you stay here for Christmas?

BOY: If that's what you want.

JO: It's what you want.

BOY: That's right.

JO: Then stay.

BOY: You naughty girl!

JO: I may as well be naughty while I've got the chance. I'll probably never see you again. I know it.

BOY: What makes you say that?

JO: I just know it. That's all. But I don't care. Stay with me

now, it's enough, it's all I want, and if you do come back
I'll still be here.

BOY: You think I'm only after one thing, don't you?

JO: I know you're only after one thing.

BOY: You're so right. [*He kisses her.*] But I will come back, I
love you.

JO: How can you say that?

BOY: Why or how I say these things I don't know, but whatever it means it's true.

JO: Anyway, after this you might not want to come back. After
all, I'm not very experienced in these little matters.

BOY: I am.

JO: Anyway, it's a bit daft for us to be talking about you
coming back before you've gone. Can I leave that hot
milk?

BOY: It would have done you good. Never mind. [*Embraces
her.*]

JO: Don't do that.

BOY: Why not?

JO: I like it.

[*Fade out. Music. Wedding bells.* HELEN'S *music. She dances
on with an assortment of fancy boxes, containing her wedding
clothes.*]

HELEN: Jo! Jo! Come on. Be sharp now.

[JO *comes on in her pyjamas. She has a heavy cold.*]

For God's sake give me a hand. I'll never be ready. What
time is it? Have a look at the church clock.

JO: A quarter past eleven, and the sun's coming out.

HELEN: Oh! Well, happy the bride the sun shines on.

JO: Yeah, and happy the corpse the rain rains on. You're not
getting married in a church, are you?

HELEN: Why, are you coming to throw bricks at us? Of
course not. Do I look all right? Pass me my fur. Oh! My
fur! Do you like it?

JO: I bet somebody's missing their cat.

HELEN: It's a wedding present from that young man of mine. He spends his money like water, you know, penny wise, pound foolish. Oh! I am excited. I feel twenty-one all over again. Oh! You would have to catch a cold on my wedding day, I was going to ask you to be my bridesmaid too.

JO: Don't talk daft.

HELEN: Where did you put my shoes? Did you clean 'em? Oh! They're on my feet. Don't stand there sniffing, Jo. Use a handkerchief.

JO: I haven't got one.

HELEN: Use this, then. What's the matter with you? What are you trying to hide?

JO: Nothing.

HELEN: Don't try to kid me. What is it? Come on, let's see.

JO: It's nothing. Let go of me. You're hurting.

HELEN: What's this?

JO: A ring.

HELEN: I can see it's a ring. Who give it to you?

JO: A friend of mine.

HELEN: Who? Come on. Tell me.

JO: You're hurting me.

[HELEN *breaks the cord and gets the ring*.]

HELEN: You should have sewn some buttons on your pyjamas if you didn't want me to see. Who give it you?

JO: My boy friend. He asked me to marry him.

HELEN: Well, you silly little bitch. You mean that lad you've been knocking about with while we've been away?

JO: Yes.

HELEN: I could choke you.

JO: You've already had a damn good try.

HELEN: You haven't known him five minutes. Has he really asked you to marry him?

JO: Yes.

HELEN: Well, thank God for the divorce courts! I suppose just because I'm getting married you think you should.

JO: Have you got the monopoly?

HELEN: You stupid little devil! What sort of a wife do you think you'd make? You're useless. It takes you all your time to look after yourself. I suppose you think you're in love. Anybody can fall in love, do you know that? But what do you know about the rest of it?

JO: Ask yourself.

HELEN: You know where that ring should be? In the ashcan with everything else. Oh! I could kill her, I could really.

JO: You don't half knock me about. I hope you suffer for it.

HELEN: I've done my share of suffering if I never do any more. Oh Jo, you're only a kid. Why don't you learn from my mistakes? It takes half your life to learn from your own.

JO: You leave me alone. Can I have my ring back, please?

HELEN: What a thing to happen just when I'm going to enjoy myself for a change.

JO: Nobody's stopping you.

HELEN: Yes, and as soon as my back's turned you'll be off with this sailor boy and ruin yourself for good.

JO: I'm already ruined.

HELEN: Yes, it's just the sort of thing you'd do. You make me sick.

JO: You've no need to worry, Helen. He's gone away. He may be back in six months, but there again, he may . . .

HELEN: Look, you're only young. Enjoy your life. Don't get trapped. Marriage can be hell for a kid.

JO: Can I have your hanky back?

HELEN: Where did you put it?

JO: This is your fault too.

HELEN: Everything's my fault. Show me your tongue.

JO: Breathing your 'flu bugs all over me.

HELEN: Yes, and your neck's red where I pulled that string.

JO: Will you get me a drink of water, Helen?

HELEN: No, have a dose of this [*Offering whisky*]. It'll do you more good. I might as well have one myself while I'm at it, mightn't I?

JO: You've emptied more bottles down your throat in the last few weeks than I would have thought possible. If you don't watch it, you'll end up an old down-and-out boozer knocking back the meths.

HELEN: It'll never come to that. The devil looks after his own, they say.

JO: He certainly takes good care of you. You look marvellous, considering.

HELEN: Considering what?

JO: The wear and tear on your soul.

HELEN: Oh well, that'll have increased its market value, won't it?

JO: Old Nick'll get you in the end.

HELEN: Thank God for that! Heaven must be the hell of a place. Nothing but repentant sinners up there, isn't it? All the pimps, prostitutes and politicians in creation trying to cash in on eternity and their little tin god. Where's my hat?

JO: Where's your husband?

HELEN: Probably drunk with his pals somewhere. He was going down to the house this morning to let some air in. Have you seen a picture of the house? Yes, you have. Do you like it? [*She peers and primps into mirror.*]

JO: It's all right if you like that sort of thing, and I don't.

HELEN: I'll like it in a few years, when it isn't so new and clean. At the moment it's like my face, unblemished! Oh look at that, every line tells a dirty story, hey?

JO: Will you tell me something before you go?

HELEN: Oh! You can read all about that in books.

JO: What was my father like?

[HELEN *turns away.*]

HELEN: Who?

JO: You heard! My father! What was he like?

HELEN: Oh! Him.

JO: Well, was he so horrible that you can't even tell me about him?

HELEN: He wasn't horrible. He was just a bit stupid, you know. Not very bright.

JO: Be serious, Helen.

HELEN: I am serious.

JO: Are you trying to tell me he was an idiot?

HELEN: He wasn't an idiot, he was just a bit – retarded.

JO: You liar!

HELEN: All right, I'm a liar.

JO: Look at me.

HELEN: Well, am I?

JO: No.

HELEN: Well, now you know.

JO: How could you give me a father like that?

HELEN: I didn't do it on purpose. How was I to know you'd materialize out of a little love affair that lasted five minutes?

JO: You never think. That's your trouble.

HELEN: I know.

JO: Was he like a . . . a real idiot?

HELEN: I've told you once. He was nice though, you know, a nice little feller!

JO: Where is he now, locked up?

HELEN: No, he's dead.

JO: Why?

HELEN: Why? Well, I mean, death's something that comes to us all, and when it does come you haven't usually got time to ask why.

JO: It's hereditary, isn't it?

HELEN: What?

JO: Madness.

HELEN: Sometimes.

JO: Am I mad?

HELEN: Decide for yourself. Oh, Jo, don't be silly. Of course you're not daft. Not more so than anybody else.

JO: Why did you have to tell me that story? Couldn't you have made something up?

HELEN: You asked for the truth and you got it for once. Now be satisfied?

JO: How could you go with a half-wit?

HELEN: He had strange eyes. You've got 'em. Everybody used to laugh at him. Go on, I'll tell you some other time.

JO: Tell me now!

HELEN: Mind my scent!

JO: Please tell me. I want to understand.

HELEN: Do you think I understand? For one night, actually it was the afternoon, I loved him. It was the first time I'd ever really been with a man . . .

JO: You were married.

HELEN: I was married to a Puritan – do you know what I mean?

JO: I think so.

HELEN: And when I met your father I was as pure and un-sullied as I fondly, and perhaps mistakenly, imagine you to be. It was the first time and though you can enjoy the second, the third, even the fourth time, there's no time like the first, it's always there. I'm off now. I've got to go and find my husband. Now don't sit here sulking all day.

JO: I was thinking.

HELEN: Well, don't think. It doesn't do you any good. I'll see you when the honeymoon's over. Come on, give us a kiss. You may as well. It's a long time since you kissed me.

JO: Keep it for him.

HELEN: I don't suppose you're sorry to see me go.

JO: I'm not sorry and I'm not glad.

HELEN: You don't know what you do want.

JO: Yes. I do. I've always known what I want.

HELEN: And when it comes your way will you recognize it?

JO: Good luck, Helen.

HELEN: I'll be seeing you. Hey! If he doesn't show up I'll be back.

JO: Good luck, Helen.

[*Exit* HELEN. *"Here comes the Bride" on the cornet.*]

Curtain

Act Two

SCENE ONE

As the curtain goes up fairground music can be heard in the distance. JO *and a boy can be heard playing together. When they enter the flat they have been playing about with a bunch of brightly coloured balloons. It is summer now and* JO'S *pregnancy is quite obvious.*

JO [*as she falls on a couch in the darkened room*]: Let me lie here and don't wake me up for a month.

GEOF: Shall I put the light on?

JO: No. Don't you dare put that light on.

GEOF: Did you enjoy the fair?

JO: Loved it. I haven't been to a fair since Christmas.

GEOF: Those roundabouts are still going. Can you hear 'em?

JO: I should be up at half past seven tomorrow morning. I'll never make it. I'll just have to be late. Anyway, why should I slave away for anybody but me? Haven't you got a home to go to, Geof?

GEOF: Of course.

JO: Well, why are you lurking about? Come in if you want to.

GEOF: Thanks.

JO: There's some biscuits and a flask of coffee in the kitchen only I'm too tired to get 'em. Aren't you hungry?

GEOF: No, but you are.

JO: That's right. Go and get 'em for me, Geof.

GEOF: Where's the kitchen?

JO: Straight on.

GEOF: I'll put the light on.

JO: No, you won't! I like this romantic half-light, it just goes with this Manchester maisonette!

GEOF: Take four paces forward, turn right, turn left, once round the gasworks and straight on up the creek. [*He bangs into a chair or table and cries or swears.*]

JO: Put a match on, you daft thing.

[GEOF *strikes a match.*]

GEOF: Ee, this place is enormous, isn't it?

JO: I know. I've got to work all day in a shoe shop and all night in a bar to pay for it. But it's mine. All mine.

GEOF: I can tell it's yours from the state it's in. No wonder you won't put the light on. Where do you keep the cups?

JO: In the sink.

GEOF: Isn't this place a bit big for one, Jo?

JO: Why? Are you thinking of moving in?

GEOF: Not likely.

JO: You are, you know. Put 'em down here. Don't you want any?

GEOF: No.

JO: Well, hand 'em over to me because I'm starved. Has your landlady thrown you out?

GEOF: Don't be silly.

JO: I've been wondering why you were so anxious to see me home. You didn't fancy sleeping under the arches, did you? Why did your landlady throw you out, Geoffrey? I'll let you stay here if you tell me.

GEOF: I was behind with the rent.

JO: That's a lie for a start.

GEOF: I don't tell lies.

JO: Come on, let's have some truth. Why did she throw you out?

GEOF: I've told you why.

JO [*switches on light*]: Come on, the truth. Who did she find you with? Your girl friend? It wasn't a man, was it?

GEOF: Don't be daft.

JO: Look, I've got a nice comfortable couch, I've even got some sheets. You can stay here if you'll tell me what you do. Go on, I've always wanted to know about people like you.

GEOF: Go to hell.

JO: I won't snigger, honest I won't. Tell me some of it, go on. I bet you never told a woman before.

GEOF: I don't go in for sensation: l confessions.

JO: I want to know what you do. I want to know why you do it. Tell me or get out.

GEOF: Right! [He goes to the door.]

JO: Geof, don't go. Don't go. Geof! I'm sorry. Please stay.

GEOF: Don't touch me.

JO: I didn't mean to hurt your feelings.

GEOF: I can't stand women at times. Let go of me.

JO: Come on, Geof. I don't care what you do.

GEOF: Thank you. May I go now, please?

JO: Please stay here Geof. I'll get those sheets and blankets.

GEOF: I can't stand people who laugh at other people. They'd get a bigger laugh if they laughed at themselves.

JO: Please stay, Geof. [She goes off for the sheets and blankets. He finds her book of drawings on the table and glances through them.]

GEOF: Are these yours?

JO: No, why? Put them down, Geof.

GEOF: Obviously they are. They're exactly like you.

JO: How do you mean?

GEOF: Well, there's no design, rhythm or purpose.

JO: Hey?

GEOF: Where's the design in that? It's all messy, isn't it? Charcoal. I don't like it.

JO: I do.

GEOF: What made you choose that for a subject?

JO: I like . . .

GEOF: They're all sentimental.

JO: Me? Sentimental?

GEOF: No. No. I don't like 'em.

JO: Do you really think they're sentimental?

GEOF: Well, look. I mean . . .

JO: I'm sorry you don't like them.

GEOF: Why don't you go to a decent school?

JO: I've never been to any school.

GEOF: You want taking in hand.

JO: No, thanks.

GEOF: Has anybody ever tried?

JO: What?

GEOF: Taking you in hand.

JO: Yes.

GEOF: What happened to him?

JO: He came in with Christmas and went out with the New Year.

GEOF: Did you like him?

JO: He was all right . . .

GEOF: Did you love him?

JO: I don't know much about love. I've never been too familiar with it. I suppose I must have loved him. They say love creates. And I'm certainly creating at the moment. I'm going to have a baby.

GEOF: I thought so. You're in a bit of a mess, aren't you?

JO: I don't care.

GEOF: You can get rid of babies before they're born, you know.

JO: I know, but I think that's terrible.

GEOF: When's it due?

JO: Reckon it up from Christmas.

GEOF: About September.

JO: Yes.

GEOF: What are you going to do? You can't be on your own.

JO: There's plenty of time.

GEOF: Got any money?

JO: Only my wages and they don't last long. By the time I've bought all I need, stockings and make-up and things, I've got nothing left.

GEOF: You can do without make-up.

JO: I can't, I look like a ghost without it.

GEOF: At your age?

JO: What's age got to do with it? Anyway, I'm not working for much longer. I'm not having everybody staring at me.

GEOF: How are you going to manage then?

JO: There's no need for you to worry about it.

GEOF: Somebody's got to. Anyway, I like you.

JO: I like you too.

GEOF: Your mother should know.

JO: Why?

GEOF: Well, she's your mother. Do you know her address?

JO: No. She was supposed to be marrying some man. They live in a big, white house somewhere.

GEOF: What sort of a woman is she?

JO: She's all sorts of woman. But she's got plenty of money.

GEOF: That's all you need to be interested in. You've got to buy all sorts of things for the baby. Clothes, a cot and a pram. Here, that teddy bear we won tonight'll come in handy, won't it? I can make things too. I'll help . . .

JO: Shut up! I'm not planning big plans for this baby or dreaming big dreams. You know what happens when you do things like that. The baby'll be born dead or daft!

GEOF: You're feeling a bit depressed, Jo.

JO: I'm feeling nothing.

GEOF: You'll be your usual self soon.

JO: And what is my usual self? My usual self is a very unusual self, Geoffrey Ingram, and don't you forget it. I'm an extraordinary person. There's only one of me like there's only one of you.

GEOF: We're unique!

JO: Young.

GEOF: Unrivalled!

JO: Smashing!

GEOF: We're bloody marvellous!

JO: Hey! Do you like beer?

GEOF: Yes.

JO: Whisky?

GEOF: Yes.

JO: Gin?

GEOF: Yes. Have you got some?

JO: No, but if I had I'd give it all to you. I'd give everything
I had to you. Here, have a biscuit. You'll like these. They
taste like dog food.

GEOF: Spratts!

JO: You look like a spratt. Jack Spratt, who'd eat no fat, his
wife would eat no lean and so between them both, you see,
they licked the platter clean. Did you enjoy that dramatic
recitation?

GEOF: Very moving.

JO: You say one.

GEOF: There was a young man of Thessaly,
      And he was wondrous wise.
      He jumped into a quickset hedge
      And scratched out both his eyes.
      And when he saw his eyes were out,
      With all his might and main
      He jumped into another hedge
      And scratched them in again.

JO: I like that. Do you know any more?

GEOF: As I was going up Pippin Hill,
      Pippin Hill was dirty.
      And there a I met a pretty miss
      And she dropped me a curtsy.
      Little miss, pretty miss,
      Blessings light upon you.
      If I had half a crown a day
      I'd gladly spend it on you.

JO: Would you?

GEOF: I would.

JO: Silly things nursery rhymes when you weigh them up.

GEOF: I like them. Do you want a cigarette?

JO: How many have you got left?

GEOF: I've got enough for one each.

JO: No, you keep 'em. They don't bother me really. I used to smoke just to annoy my mother. What's that?

GEOF: A free gift coupon.

JO: Everything you buy lately has a free gift coupon in it. It's coming to something when they have to bribe the public to buy their stuff. What's this one for?

GEOF: There's a whole list of things to send for if you have enough coupons. Hee, there's even a car, smoke forty thousand cigarettes a day for the next ten thousand years and you'll get a Lagonda.

JO: What's that?

GEOF: A car.

JO: A nice car?

GEOF: A wonderful car.

JO: I'll buy you one for Christmas. If you ask me nice I'll buy you two.

GEOF: Thanks.

JO: Oh! I'm tired. This couch isn't going to be very comfortable, is it?

GEOF: It'll do.

JO: What are you going to sleep in?

GEOF: My shirt!

JO: I'm that tired! I haven't the energy to get myself to bed. You won't sleep very well on this couch, Geof.

GEOF: It's all right. Beggars can't be choosers.

JO: We're both beggars. A couple of degenerates.

GEOF: The devil's own!

JO [*she goes to bed.* GEOF *starts to undress*]: Hey! You'd better turn that light out, or I might be after you. [*He turns the*

light out and then gets into bed. She begins to sing the song
"Black Boy" as she lies on her bed.]
Black boy, black boy, don't you lie to me.
Where did you stay last night?
In the pines, in the pines where the sun never shines,
I shivered the whole night through.

GEOF: Jo!

JO: Yes.

GEOF: What was that boy like?

JO: Which boy?

GEOF: You know.

JO: Oh! Him. He wasn't a bit like you. He could sing and
dance and he was as black as coal.

GEOF: A black boy?

JO: From darkest Africa! A Prince.

GEOF: A what?

JO: A Prince, son of a chieftain.

GEOF: I'll bet he was too.

JO: Prince Ossini!

GEOF: What was he doing here?

JO: He was a male nurse in the Navy.

GEOF: Do you wish he was still here?

JO: Not really. I think I've had enough. I'm sick of love. That's
why I'm letting you stay here. You won't start anything.

GEOF: No, I don't suppose I will.

JO: You'd better not. I hate love.

GEOF: Do you, Jo?

JO: Yes, I do.

GEOF: Good night.

JO: Good night.

GEOF: You needn't lock the bedroom door.

JO: I'm in bed. Geoffrey! Geoffrey!

GEOF: What do you want?

JO: What time have you got to be up in the morning?

GEOF: I don't go to school tomorrow. I'll stay here and clear

this place up a bit. And make you a proper meal. Now go
to sleep, hey?

JO: Geoffrey!

GEOF: What's wrong now?

JO [*laughing*]: You're just like a big sister to me.

[*Music to black out. Then quick as lights go up. Waking,* GEOF
dances and goes off with bedclothes. JO *dances off.* GEOF
*dances in with props for the next scene, which in reality
would be a month or two later.* GEOF *is cutting out a baby's
gown.* JO *wanders about the room.*]

JO: God! It's hot.

GEOF: I know it's hot.

JO: I'm so restless.

GEOF: Oh, stop prowling about.

JO: This place stinks. [*Goes over to the door. Children are heard
singing in the street.*] That river, it's the colour of lead. Look
at that washing, it's dirty, and look at those filthy children.

GEOF: It's not their fault.

JO: It's their parents' fault. There's a little boy over there and
his hair, honestly, it's walking away. And his ears. Oh!
He's a real mess! He never goes to school. He just sits on
that front doorstep all day. I think he's a bit deficient.

[*The children's voices die away. A tugboat hoots.*]

His mother ought not to be allowed.

GEOF: Who?

JO: His mother. Think of all the harm she does, having children.

GEOF: Sit down and read a book, Jo.

JO: I can't.

GEOF: Be quiet then. You're getting on my nerves. [*Suddenly
she yells and whirls across the room.*]

JO: Whee! Come on rain. Come on storm. It kicked me,
Geof. It kicked me!

GEOF: What?

JO: It kicked me. [GEOF *runs to her and puts his head on her belly*.]

GEOF: Will it do it again?

JO: It shows it's alive anyway. Come on, baby, let's see what big sister's making for us.

GEOF: Put it down.

JO: What a pretty little dress.

GEOF: It's got to wear something. You can't just wrap it up in a bundle of newspaper.

JO: And dump it on a doorstep. How did Geoffrey find out the measurements?

GEOF: Babies are born to the same size more or less.

JO: Oh, no, they're not. Some are thin scrappy things and others are huge and covered in rolls of fat.

GEOF: Shut up, Jo, it sounds revolting.

JO: They are revolting. I hate babies.

GEOF: I thought you'd change. Motherhood is supposed to come natural to women.

JO: It comes natural to you, Geoffrey Ingram. You'd make somebody a wonderful wife. What were you talking about to that old mare downstairs?

GEOF: I was giving her the rent. I got my grant yesterday.

JO: You're as thick as thieves, you two.

GEOF: She's going to make the baby a cradle.

JO: What?

GEOF: You know, she makes wicker baskets.

JO: A wicker basket!

GEOF: It's the best we can do, unless you want to go down to the river plaiting reeds.

JO: I don't want her poking her nose into my affairs.

GEOF: You're glad enough to have me dancing attendance on you.

JO: Only because I thought you'd leave me alone. Why don't you leave me alone? [*She cries and flings herself down on the couch*.] I feel like throwing myself in the river.

GEOF: I wouldn't do that. It's full of rubbish.

JO: Well that's all I am, isn't it?

GEOF: Stop pitying yourself.

JO: Don't jump down my throat.

GEOF: How much longer is this going on?

JO: What?

GEOF: Your present performance.

JO: Nobody asked you to stay here. You moved in on me, remember, remember? If you don't like it you can get out, can't you? But you wouldn't do that, would you, Geoffrey? You've no confidence in yourself, have you? You're afraid the girls might laugh . . .

GEOF: Read that book and shut up. When the baby comes, if it ever does, you won't know one end of it from the other.

JO: *Looking After Baby*. Isn't that nice? Three months, exercises, constipation. Four months, relaxation. It even tells you how to wash nappies. How lovely. There's a little job for you, Geoffrey.

GEOF: Drink that. [*He hands her a glass of milk.*]

JO [*flirting with him*]: Does it tell you how to feed babies, Geoffrey?

GEOF: Even you know that.

JO: I know about that way, breast feeding, but I'm not having a little animal nibbling away at me, it's cannibalistic. Like being eaten alive.

GEOF: Stop trying to be inhuman. It doesn't suit you.

JO: I mean it. I hate motherhood.

GEOF: Well, whether you hate it or not you've got it coming to you so you might as well make a good job of it.

JO: I've got toothache.

GEOF: I've got bloody heartache!

JO: I think you'd like everybody to think this baby's yours, wouldn't you, Geoffrey?

GEOF: Not likely.

JO: After all, you don't show much sign of coming fatherhood, do you? You like babies, don't you, Geof?

GEOF: Yes, I do.

JO [*coquettes with him*]: Geoffrey, have you got any of that toothache cure?

[*He moves away.*]

Geoffrey, have you got any of that toothache cure?

GEOF: The only cure for the toothache is a visit to the dentist. Drink your milk.

JO: I hate milk [*She looks out of the window.*] I never thought I'd still be here in the summer. [*She puts her arms round* GEOF *playfully.*] Would you like to be the father of my baby, Geoffrey?

GEOF: Yes, I would.

[JO *stands in the doorway. The children can be heard singing again.*]

What time is it?

JO: Half-past four by the church clock. Why do you stay here, Geof?

GEOF: Someone's got to look after you. You can't look after yourself.

JO: I think there's going to be a storm. Look at that sky. It's nearly black. And you can hear the kids playing, right over there on the croft.

[*A silence in the room: we hear the children singing.*]

GEOF: What would you say if I started something?

JO: Eh!

GEOF: I said what would you say if I started something?

JO: In my condition I'd probably faint.

GEOF: No, I mean after.

JO: I don't want you.

GEOF: Am I repulsive to you?

JO: You're nothing to me. I'm everything to myself.

GEOF: No, you're not. You're going to need me after.

JO: I won't be here after.

GEOF: Do you still think he might come back?

JO: I've forgotten him.

[*She turns towards him, he to her.*]

GEOF: You do need me, Jo, don't you?

JO: Let go of me. You're squeezing my arm.

GEOF: I've never kissed a girl.

JO: That's your fault.

GEOF: Let me kiss you.

JO: Let go of me. Leave me alone.

[*She struggles but he kisses her.*]

GEOF: How was that for first time?

JO: Practise on somebody else.

GEOF: I didn't mean to hurt you.

JO: Look Geof, I like you, I like you very much, but I don't enjoy all this panting and grunting ...

GEOF: Marry me, Jo.

JO: Don't breathe all over me like that, you sound like a horse. I'm not marrying anybody.

GEOF: I wouldn't ask you to do anything you didn't want to do.

JO: Yes, you would.

GEOF: Jo, I don't mind that you're having somebody else's baby. What you've done, you've done. What I've done, I've done.

JO: I like you, Geof, but I don't want to marry you.

GEOF: Oh, all right. Anyway, I don't suppose I could live up to that black beast of a prince of yours. I bet you didn't struggle when he made love to you.

JO: It might have been better if I had.

GEOF [*he gives her a bar of chocolate*]: Have some chocolate.

JO: Thanks. Do you want some?

GEOF: No.

JO: Go on.

GEOF: I said no.

JO: You like strawberry cream.

GEOF: I don't want any, Jo. I've made my mind up.

JO: Don't be daft, have some chocolate.

GEOF: No ... [*She gives a piece of chocolate to him just the same.*]

JO: I think it would be best if you left this place, Geof. I don't think it's doing you any good being here with me all the time.

GEOF: I know that, but I couldn't go away now.

JO: You'll have to go some time. We can't stay together like this for ever.

GEOF: I'd sooner be dead than away from you.

JO: You say that as if you mean it.

GEOF: I do mean it.

JO: Why?

GEOF: Before I met you I didn't care one way or the other – I didn't care whether I lived or died. But now ...

JO: I think I'll go and lie down. [*She goes to bed and lies across it.*]

GEOF: There's no need for me to go, Jo. You said yourself you didn't want anybody else here and I'm only interested in you. We needn't split up need we, Jo?

JO: I don't suppose so.

[*Music. Enter* HELEN.]

HELEN: Jo! Your beloved old lady's arrived. Well, where is she, Romeo?

GEOF: Don't tell her I came for you.

HELEN: What? Don't mumble.

GEOF: I said don't tell her I came for you.

HELEN: All right, all right. This place hasn't changed much, has it? Still the same old miserable hole. Well, where's the lady in question?

GEOF: In there.

HELEN: What, lazing in bed, as usual? Come on, get up; plenty

of girls in your condition have to go out to work and take
care of a family. Come on, get up.

JO: What blew you in?

HELEN: Let's have a look at you.

JO: Who told you about me?

HELEN: Nobody.

JO: How did you get to know then?

HELEN: Come on, aren't you going to introduce me to your
boy friend? Who is he?

JO: My boy friend. Oh, it's all right, we're so decent we're
almost dead. I said who told you about me?

HELEN: Does it matter?

JO: I told you to keep out of my affairs, Geoffrey. I'm not having anybody running my life for me. What do you think
you're running? A "Back to Mother" movement?

GEOF: Your mother has a right to know.

JO: She's got no rights where I'm concerned.

HELEN: Oh, leave him alone. You're living off him, by all
accounts.

JO: Who've you been talking to? That old hag downstairs?

HELEN: I didn't need to talk to her. The whole district knows
what's been going on here.

JO: And what has been going on?

HELEN: I suppose you think you can hide yourself away in this
chicken run, don't you? Well, you can't. Everybody knows.

GEOF: She won't go out anywhere, not even for a walk and a
bit of fresh air. That's why I came to you.

HELEN: And what do you think I can do about it? In any case,
bearing a child doesn't place one under an obligation to it.

GEOF: I should have thought it did.

HELEN: Well, you've got another think coming. If she won't
take care of herself that's her lookout. And don't stand
there looking as if it's my fault.

GEOF: It's your grandchild.

HELEN: Oh, shut up, you put years on me. Anyway, I'm having

nothing to do with it. She's more than I can cope with, always has been.

GEOF: That's obvious.

HELEN: And what's your part in this little Victorian melodrama? Nursemaid?

JO: Serves you right for bringing her here, Geof.

HELEN: It's a funny-looking set-up to me.

JO: It's our business.

HELEN: Then don't bring me into it. Where's the loving father? Distinguished by his absence, I suppose.

JO: That's right.

HELEN [to GEOF]: Did she hear any more of him?

JO: No, she didn't.

HELEN: When I'm talking to the organ grinder I don't expect the monkey to answer.

JO: I could get him back tomorrow if I wanted to.

HELEN: Well, that's nice to know. He certainly left you a nice Christmas box. It did happen at Christmas, I suppose? When the cat's away.

GEOF: You've been away a long time.

HELEN: Oh, you shut up. Sling your hook!

JO: Will you keep out of this, Geoffrey?

HELEN: Well, come on, let's have a look at you. [JO turns away.] What's up? We're all made the same, aren't we?

JO: Yes we are.

HELEN: Well then. Can you cut the bread on it yet? [JO turns.] Yes, you're carrying it a bit high, aren't you? Are you going to the clinic regularly? Is she working?

GEOF: No, I told you, she doesn't like people looking at her.

HELEN: Do you think people have got nothing better to do than look at you?

JO: Leave me alone.

HELEN: She'd be better off working than living off you like a little bloodsucker.

GEOF: She doesn't live off me.

JO: No, we share everything, see! We're communists too.

HELEN: That's his influence I suppose.

JO: Get out of here. I won't go out if I don't want to. It's nothing to do with you. Get back to your fancy man or your husband, or whatever you like to call him.

[HELEN *begins to chase her*.]

Aren't you afraid he'll run off and leave you if you let him out of your sight?

HELEN: I'll give you such a bloody good hiding in a minute, if you're not careful. That's what you've gone short of!

JO: Don't show yourself up for what you are!

HELEN: You couldn't wait, could you? Now look at the mess you've landed yourself in.

JO: I'll get out of it, without your help.

HELEN: You had to throw yourself at the first man you met, didn't you?

JO: Yes, I did, that's right.

HELEN: You're man mad.

JO: I'm like you.

HELEN: You know what they're calling you round here? A silly little whore!

JO: Well, they all know where I get it from too.

HELEN: Let me get hold of her! I'll knock her bloody head round!

JO: You should have been locked up years ago, with my father.

HELEN: Let me get hold of her!

GEOF: Please, Jo, Helen, Jo, please!

HELEN: I should have got rid of you before you were born.

JO: I wish you had done. You did with plenty of others, I know.

HELEN: I'll kill her. I'll knock the living daylights out of her.

GEOF: Helen, stop it, you will kill her!

JO: If you don't get out of here I'll ... jump out of the window.

[*There is a sudden lull.*]

GEOF [*yelling*]: Will you stop shouting, you two?

HELEN: We enjoy it.

GEOF: Helen!

HELEN: Now you're going to listen to a few home truths, my girl.

JO: We've had enough home truths!

HELEN: All right, you thought you knew it all before, didn't you? But you came a cropper. Now it's "poor little Josephine, the tragedy queen, hasn't life been hard on her". Well, you fell down, you get up ... nobody else is going to carry you about. Oh, I know you've got this pansified little freak to lean on, but what good will that do you?

JO: Leave Geof out of it!

HELEN: Have you got your breath back? Because there's some more I've got to get off my chest first.

JO: You don't half like the sound of your own voice.

GEOF: If I'd known you were going to bully her like this I'd never have asked you to come here.

HELEN: You can clear off! Take your simpering little face out of it!

JO: Yes, buzz off, Geof! Well, who brought her here? I told you what sort of a woman she was. Go and ... go and make a cup of tea.

[*He goes.*]

HELEN: Look at your arms. They're like a couple of stalks! You look like a ghost warmed up. And who gave you that haircut, him? Don't sit there sulking.

JO: I thought it was the tea break.

HELEN: I didn't come here to quarrel.

JO: No?

HELEN: I brought you some money.

JO: You know what you can do with that.

HELEN: All right! You've said your piece. Money doesn't

grow on trees. I'll leave it on the table. Have you been collecting your maternity benefit or . . .

JO: Or are you too idle to walk down to the post office? Don't be daft! I'm not entitled to it. I haven't been earning long enough.

HELEN: You've no need to go short of anything.

JO: It's taken you a long time to come round to this, hasn't it?

HELEN: What?

JO: The famous mother-love act.

HELEN: I haven't been able to sleep for thinking about you since he came round to our house.

JO: And your sleep mustn't be disturbed at any cost.

HELEN: There'll be money in the post for you every week from now on.

JO: Until you forget.

HELEN: I don't forget things; It's just that I can't remember anything. I'm going to see you through this whether you like it or not. After all I am . . .

JO: After all you are my mother! You're a bit late remembering that, aren't you? You walked through that door with that man and didn't give me a second thought.

HELEN: Why didn't you tell me?

JO: You should have known. You're nothing to me.

[PETER appears.]

PETER: What the hell's going on? Do you expect me to wait in the filthy street all night?

HELEN: I told you to stay outside.

PETER: Don't point your bloody finger at me.

HELEN: I said I'd only be a few minutes and I've only been a few minutes. Now come on, outside!

PETER: Ah! The erring daughter. There she is. [Sings.] "Little Josephine, you're a big girl now." Where d'you keep the whisky?

HELEN: They haven't got any. Now, come on.

PETER [*seeing* GEOF]: What's this, the father? Oh Christ, no!

GEOF: Who's he?

HELEN: President of the local Temperance Society!

PETER [*singing*]: "Who's got a bun in the oven? Who's got a cake in the stove?"

HELEN: Leave her alone.

PETER: Oh, go to hell!

JO: I've got nothing to say . . .

PETER: Go on, have your blasted family reunion, don't mind me! [*Notices* GEOF *again*.] Who's this? Oh, of course! Where are the drinks, Lana? [*He falls into the kitchen, singing.*] "Getting to know you, getting to know all about you . . ."

HELEN: Jo, come on . . .

[*There is a loud crash in the kitchen.*]

And the light of the world shone upon him.

[PETER *enters.*]

PETER: Cheer up, everybody. I am back. Who's the lily? Look at Helen, well, if she doesn't look like a bloody unrestored oil painting. What's the matter everybody? Look at the sour-faced old bitch! Well, are you coming for a few drinks or aren't you?

HELEN: The pubs aren't open yet.

JO: Do you mind getting out of here?

PETER: Shut your mouth, bubble belly! Before I shut it for you. Hey! [*To* GEOF.] Mary, come here. Did I ever tell you about the chappie who married his mother by mistake?

JO: I said get him out of here, Helen. His breath smells.

HELEN: I can't carry him out, can I?

PETER: His name was Oedipus, he was a Greek I think. Well, the old bag turned out to be his mother . . .

HELEN: Shut up, Peter, for God's sake!

PETER: So he scratched out both his eyes.

HELEN: Cut the dirty stories!

PETER: But I only scratched out one of mine. Well, are you coming or not?

HELEN: I'm not.

PETER: Well, is anybody coming for a few drinks? You staying with the ladies, Jezebel?

GEOF: Listen, mister, this is my friend's flat . . .

PETER: And what do you do, Cuddles? Don't worry, I know this district. Look at Helen, isn't she a game old bird? Worn out on the beat but she's still got a few good strokes left.

HELEN: Get out of here, you drunken sot.

PETER: Now I told you to moderate your language. What's this? Giving my money away again?

HELEN: Take your bloody money and get out!

PETER: Thank you.

HELEN: You dirty bastard!

PETER: You should have heard her the other night. You know what happened? Her wandering boy returned. He hadn't been home for two weeks and do you know why? He picked up a couple of grapefruit on a thirty-two bust, rich, young and juicy . . . hey! Where's the smallest room?

GEOF: This way.

PETER: And she went off the deep end. [*Sings as he goes. Another crash offstage.*]

HELEN [*to* GEOF]: You'd better go with him or Lord knows where he'll end up.

GEOF: I hope the landlady hasn't heard him.

HELEN: Cigarette?

JO: No. Yes, I will. I'll keep it for Geof.

HELEN: You'd better have the whole bloody packet if you're in such a state.

JO: Well, he couldn't hold it any more, could he?

HELEN: No one could hold that much.

JO: How long has he been like this?

HELEN: What does that boy friend of yours do for a living?

JO: He's an art student. I suppose that's what's been keeping you occupied?

HELEN: An art student. I might have known. Does he live here?

JO: Why should I answer your questions? You never answer any of mine.

HELEN: Look at you! Why don't you take a bit of pride in yourself? Grow your hair properly?

JO: Look at you. Look what your pride in yourself has done for you.

HELEN: Come and stay with me, Jo; there's a nice room and plenty of food.

JO: No, thanks.

HELEN: You prefer to stay in this hole with that pansified little freak?

GEOF: Shall I go?

HELEN: I didn't know you'd come.

JO: Would you go and live with her if you were me, Geof?

GEOF: No, I don't think I would.

JO: Neither would anybody in their right mind.

GEOF: She always said you were a pretty rotten sort of woman. I thought she was exaggerating.

HELEN: Look, can't you get it into your stupid head that I'm offering you a decent home?

[PETER *enters, more sober, more unpleasant.*]

PETER: Bloody cockroaches are playing leapfrog in there.

HELEN: Look, I'll tell you again, in front of him, my home is yours.

PETER: Ah! Shut up!

HELEN: I'll take care of you and see you through it.

JO: The time to have taken care of me was years ago, when I couldn't take care of myself.

HELEN: All right, but we're talking about here and now. When

I really set out to take care of somebody I usually do the
job properly.

JO: So I see.

PETER: I'm not having that bloody slut at our place. I'll tell
you that for nothing.

HELEN: Take no notice. The house is half mine.

PETER: Like hell it is. I could throw you out tomorrow.

JO: I don't think . . .

PETER: And don't bring that little fruitcake parcel either!
[*Mumbles.*] I can't stand the sight of him. Can't stand 'em
at any price.

HELEN: Oh, keep out of it. Jo, I can't bear to think of you
sitting here in this dump!

PETER: Neither can I. Now let's get going.

HELEN: The whole district's rotten, it's not fit to live in.

PETER: Let's go before we grow old sitting here.

HELEN: Shut up, the pubs will be open in ten minutes.

PETER: You're wrong there. [*Looking at his watch.*] They're
open now. What time do you make it?

GEOF: There's one thing about this district, the people in it
aren't rotten. Anyway, I think she's happier here with me
than in that dazzling white house you're supposed to be
so . . .

PETER: Dazzling bunch of bul . . . lot of bloody outsiders,
no class at all. What's the time anyway?

HELEN [*to* GEOF]: You shut up! I know what she needs if she's
not going to finish up in a box.

PETER: What's the time by your watch, sonny?

GEOF: It's never been right since it last went wrong.

PETER: Neither have I. How long are we going to sit around
in this room? I don't like the smell of unwashed bodies,
woman. I dragged you out of the gutter once. If you want
to go back there it's all the same to me. I'm not having this
shower at any price. I'm telling you for the last time because
I'm getting out of it. Stay if you want, it's all the same to

me; it's your own bloody level. Well, are you coming or not?

HELEN: I'm not.

PETER: I said are you coming?

HELEN: And I said I'm not.

PETER: Well, you can just go and take a flying flip out of the window. [*He goes.*]

HELEN: I'll ... I'll ... would you sooner I stayed here with you?

JO: No, thanks.

PETER: Helen ... [*Calling*]. ... come on!

HELEN: I'll send you some money.

JO: Keep it. You might need it.

PETER: Helen!

HELEN: Go to ...

PETER: Are you coming?

HELEN [*yelling*]: Yes. [*To* GEOF.] See that she goes to the clinic regularly and be sure she gets enough to eat.

GEOF: She has been doing that.

HELEN: I'll see you around. [*She goes.*]

JO: Well, here endeth the third lesson.

GEOF: At least she left you some money. We can get some ...

JO: He took it back. I got you a cigarette though, love.

GEOF: Oh, smashing! I was out.

[*Music. They dance together. Fade out.*]

SCENE TWO

GEOFFREY *dances in with a mop and bucket and begins to clean the place.* JO *dances back and sits on the table reading. She is wearing a long white housecoat and again, in reality, months have passed between this and the previous scene. Music out.*

JO: "Ninth month, everything should now be in readiness for the little stranger." Where did you find this book, Geoffrey? It reads like *Little Women*.

GEOF: I got it for fourpence off a book barrow.

JO: You've got terrible tendencies, haven't you?

GEOF: How do you mean?

JO: You like everything to be just that little bit out of date, don't you? Clothes, books, women.

GEOF: You've got no choice, have you? I mean you all start by living in the past. Well look, it's all around you, isn't it?

JO: I wonder if we ever catch up with ourselves?

GEOF: I don't know.

JO: Now you're a real Edwardian, aren't you?

GEOF: What's that?

JO: A proper Ted! And me, I'm contemporary.

GEOF: God help us!

JO: I really am, aren't I? I really do live at the same time as myself, don't I?

GEOF: Do you mind? I've just done all that. Oh come on! Get off!

[*He pushes her with the mop.*]

JO: Hey, hey!

GEOF: Women!

JO: You haven't noticed my home dressmaking.

GEOF: No. I've been trying to ignore it. What is it?

JO: A house-coat.

GEOF: It looks more like a badly tailored shroud.

JO: What the well-dressed expectant mother is wearing this year. I feel wonderful. Aren't I enormous?

GEOF: You're clever, aren't you?

JO: What's in the oven, Geoffrey?

GEOF: You what?

JO: What's cooking?

GEOF: A cake.

JO: Mm, you're wonderful, aren't you?

GEOF: Pretty good.

JO: I know, you make everything work. The stove goes, now we eat. You've reformed me, some of the time at any rate.

[GEOFFREY *shifts the sofa. There is old rubbish and dirt under it.*]

GEOF: Oh, Jo!

JO: I wondered where that had got to.

GEOF: Now you know. It's disgusting, it really is.

JO: Oh Geof, the bulbs I brought with me!

GEOF: Haven't you shifted the sofa since then?

JO: They never grew.

GEOF: No, I'm not surprised.

JO: They're dead. It makes you think, doesn't it?

GEOF: What does?

JO: You know, some people like to take out an insurance policy, don't they?

GEOF: I'm a bit young for you to take out one on me.

JO: No. You know, they like to pray to the Almighty just in case he turns out to exist when they snuff it.

GEOF [*brushing under the sofa*]: Well, I never think about it. You come, you go, it's simple.

JO: It's not, it's chaotic—a bit of love, a bit of lust and there you are. We don't ask for life, we have it thrust upon us.

GEOF: What's frightened you? Have you been reading the newspapers?

JO: No, I never do. Hold my hand, Geof.

GEOF: Do you mind? Halfway through this?

JO: Hold my hand.

[*He does.*]

GEOF: Hey, Jo. Come on, silly thing, it's all right. Come on there.

JO: You've got nice hands, hard. You know I used to try and hold my mother's hands, but she always used to pull them away from me. So silly really. She had so much love for everyone else, but none for me.

GEOF: If you don't watch it, you'll turn out exactly like her.

JO: I'm not like her at all.

GEOF: In some ways you are already, you know.

[*She pushes his hand away.*]

Can I go now?

JO: Yes.

GEOF: Thank you very much! [*He is pushing the couch back into position.*]

JO: "And he took up his bed and walked." You can stay here if you tell me what you do. Do you remember, Geoffrey? I used to think you were such an interesting, immoral character before I knew you. I thought you were like that . . . for one thing.

[GEOFFREY *chases her with the mop all through this speech.*]

You're just like an old woman really. You just unfold your bed, kiss me good night and sing me to sleep. Hey, what's the matter? Don't you like living here with me?

GEOF: It has its lighter moments, but on the whole it's a pretty trying prospect.

JO: Why do you wear black shirts? They make you look like a spiv.

GEOF: They do, Jo, but I can't be too particular. Good clothes cost money.

JO: Well, I weigh in with my share, don't I? That's a nice little job you got me, retouching those bloody photographs. What was it supposed to do, prove I was the artistic type? Of course we can't all be art students, going to our expensive art schools, nursing our little creative genius.

GEOF: Must you shout?

JO: I'm Irish.

GEOF: Never mind, it's not your fault.

JO [*laughing*]: I like you.

GEOF: Do you like me more than you don't like me or don't you like me more than you do?

JO: Now you're being Irish.

GEOF: Fine Irishwoman you are. Where did your ancestors fall, in the Battle of Salford Town Hall?

JO: My mother's father was Irish.

GEOF: You'll find any excuse.

JO: And she had me by an Irishman—the village idiot, from what I can make out.

GEOF: What do you mean?

JO: A frolic in a hay loft one afternoon. You see her husband thought sex was dirty, and only used the bed for sleeping in. So she took to herself an idiot. She said he'd got eyes like me.

GEOF: Are you making it up?

JO: He lived in a twilight land, my daddy. The land of the daft.

GEOF: Did she tell you all this?

JO: Yes.

GEOF: I'm not surprised. It sounds like Ibsen's *Ghosts*. I don't know where Helen gets them from, I don't really.

JO: I had to drag it out of her. She didn't want to tell me.

GEOF: That doesn't mean to say it's the truth. Do people ever tell the truth about themselves?

JO: Why should she want to spin me a yarn like that?

GEOF: She likes to make an effect.

JO: Like me?

GEOF: You said it. You only have to let your hair grow for a week for Helen to think you're a cretin.

JO: What?

GEOF: I said you've only got to let your hair grow for a week for Helen to think you're a cretin. She always looks at me as though I should be put away for treatment, doesn't she?

JO: Yes.

GEOF: I know, you don't have to tell me! Have you been worrying about that all these months?

JO: No.

GEOF: You have.

JO: I haven't.

GEOF: Well, I didn't think you could be so daft. Can you see Helen going out with a real loony!

JO: Well, now you put it like that, no, I can't!

GEOF: No, neither can—I don't know. Anyway, who knows who are the fools and the wise men in this world?

JO: I wouldn't be surprised if all the sane ones weren't in the bin.

GEOF: You're probably right. Anyway everyone knows you're as cracked as an old bedbug.

JO [*laughing*]: Thanks, Geof. You know, you're a cure.

GEOF: I used to be a patrol leader in the Boy Scouts.

JO: So long as you weren't Scoutmaster! You know, I wish she was here all the same.

GEOF: Why? You'd only quarrel. You know you always say you hate the sight of her.

JO: I do.

GEOF: Well then.

JO: She must know my time has almost come. When do your exams finish?

GEOF: On Thursday.

JO: I wonder which day it'll be? Put your arms round me, Geof. I don't want you to be worried while your exams are on.

GEOF: Then you shouldn't have asked me to put my arms round you, should you?

JO: Ah well, it doesn't matter if you fail. In this country the more you know the less you earn.

GEOF: Yes, you're probably right. I've got something for you. Oh Jo, I'm daft at times.

JO: I know that. I was wondering what it was.

GEOF [*from his pack he takes a life-sized doll*]: There—isn't it nice? I thought you could practise a few holds on it over

the weekend. You've got to be able to establish your
superiority over the little devils. I don't know where that
goes. There, look, isn't it good?

JO [*seeing the doll*]: The colour's wrong.

GEOF: Jo.

JO: The colour's wrong. [*Suddenly and violently flinging the
doll to the ground.*] I'll bash its brains out. I'll kill it. I don't
want his baby, Geof. I don't want to be a mother. I don't
want to be a woman.

GEOF: Don't say that, Jo.

JO: I'll kill it when it comes, Geoff, I'll kill it.

GEOF: Do you want me to go out and find that chap and bring
him back? Is that what you want?

JO: I don't want that. I don't want any man.

GEOF: Well, if you're going to feel like that about it you might
as well have it adopted. I thought you'd feel differently as
time went on.

JO: I won't.

GEOF: Perhaps you will when you see the baby.

JO: No, I won't.

GEOF: Do you still love him?

JO: I don't know. He was only a dream I had. You know, he
could sing and he was so tender. Every Christmas Helen
used to go off with some boy friend or other and leave me
all on my own in some sordid digs, but last Christmas I
had him.

GEOF: Your black prince.

JO: What was his name?

GEOF: Prince Ossini.

JO: No, it was Jimmie!

GEOF: Oh well, the dream's gone, but the baby's real enough.

JO: My mother always used to say you remember the first time
all your life, but until this moment I'd forgotten it.

GEOF: Do you remember when I asked you to marry me?

JO: Yes.

GEOF: Do you?

JO: No. What did I say?

GEOF: You just went and lay on the bed.

JO: And you didn't go and follow me, did you?

GEOF: No.

JO: You see, it's not marrying love between us, thank God.

GEOF: You mean you just like having me around till your next prince comes along?

JO: No.

GEOF: Oh well, you need somebody to love you while you're looking for someone to love.

JO: Oh Geof, you'd make a funny father. You are a funny little man. I mean that. You're unique.

GEOF: Am I?

JO: I always want to have you with me because I know you'll never ask anything from me. Where are you going?

[GEOFFREY goes to the kitchen.]

GEOF: To see the cake.

[JO follows him.]

JO: I'll set the cups and we'll have a celebration, then you'll have to study for your exams. It's a bit daft talking about getting married, isn't it? We're already married. We've been married for a thousand years.

[They march in together from the kitchen, he with the cake, she with the tea things.]

GEOF [putting it down]: Here, look at that. What are you going to call it?

JO: What, the cake?

GEOF [laughing]: No, Jo, the baby.

JO: I think I'll give it to you, Geof. You like babies, don't you? I might call it Number One. It'll always be number one to itself.

[HELEN enters, loaded with baggage as in Act One, Scene One.]

HELEN: Anybody at home? Well, I'm back. You see, I couldn't stay away, could I? There's some flowers for you, Jo. The barrows are smothered in them. Oh! How I carried that lot from the bus stop I'll never know. The old place looks a bit more cheerful, doesn't it? I say, there's a nice homely smell. Have you been doing a bit of baking? I'll tell you one thing, it's a lovely day for flitting.

JO: Would you like a cup of tea, Helen?

HELEN: Have you got anything stronger? Oh no, course you haven't! Go on, I'll have a cup with you. Let's have a look at you, love. I arrived just in time, by the look of things, didn't I? How are you, love? Everything straightforward? Been having your regular check-up and doing all them exercises and all the things they go in for nowadays? That's a good girl. Have you got everything packed?

JO: Packed?

HELEN: Yes.

JO: But I'm not going into hospital.

HELEN: You're not having it here, are you?

GEOF: Yes, she didn't want to go away.

HELEN: Oh my God, is he still here? I thought he would be.

GEOF: Do you want a piece of cake, Jo?

JO: Yes, please.

HELEN: You can't have a baby in this dump. Why don't you use a bit of sense for once and go into hospital? They've got everything to hand there. I mean, sometimes the first one can be a bit tricky.

GEOF: There's going to be nothing tricky about it; it's going to be perfectly all right, isn't it, Jo?

HELEN: Who do you think you are, the Flying Doctor?

JO: Look, I've made up my mind I want to have it here. I don't like hospitals.

HELEN: Have you ever been in a hospital?

JO: No.

HELEN: Well, how do you know what it's like? Oo! Give me a cup of tea quick.

GEOF: Oh well, we've got a district nurse coming in.

HELEN: Oh my God, my feet are killing me. How I got that lot from the bus stop I'll never know.

JO: Well what are you lugging all the cases about for?

HELEN: I've come to look after you. It's just as well, by the look of things. [*Whispers to* JO.]

JO: Well, it's going to be a bit crowded, you know. Is your husband coming and all? Is he moving in too?

HELEN: There wouldn't be much room for two of us on that couch, would there?

JO: That's Geoffrey's bed.

GEOF: It's all right, Jo, I don't mind moving out.

JO: For Heaven's sake, you don't have to start wilting away as soon as she barges in.

GEOF: I don't.

HELEN: I could do with a drink.

JO: Start barging around just like a bull in a china shop.

HELEN: I've got some lovely things for the baby, Jo. Where did I put them? Where's that other case, Jo? Oh!

GEOF: Jo, will you sit down. I'll get it.

HELEN: Look, love. I've come here to talk to my daughter. Can you make yourself scarce for a bit?

GEOF: I've got to go, we need some things for the weekend.

JO: You don't have to let her push you around.

GEOF: I don't.

HELEN: Oh I do wish he wouldn't mumble. It does get on my nerves. What's he saying?

GEOF: Where's my pack?

JO: What a couple of old women.

GEOF: Look here, Jo!

JO: Look, just a minute will you. I ... look I ... there's nothing ...

GEOF: How can I stay ...

HELEN: Come here. How long is he going to stick around here. Bloody little pansy . . .

JO: Look, if you're going to insult Geof . . .

HELEN: I'm not insulting him.

JO: Yes you are.

HELEN: I'm not. I just don't like his style, that's all.

GEOF: It's all right, Mrs. Smith . . .

HELEN: Look, love, I just want five minutes alone with her. Do you mind? Is it too much to ask?

GEOF: Do you want any cotton wool?

HELEN: Good God, does he knit an' all?

JO: You don't have to go.

GEOF: Jo, I've got to go, I'll only be a couple of minutes.

JO: There's plenty of stuff in the kitchen. Now look . . .

[GEOFFREY *goes*.]

HELEN: You don't mean to tell me he's really gone?

JO: Now that you've been rude to my friend . . .

HELEN: What an arty little freak! I wasn't rude to him. I never said a word. I never opened my mouth.

JO: Look, he's the only friend I've got, as a matter of fact.

HELEN: Jo! I thought you could find yourself something more like a man.

JO: Why were you so nasty to him?

HELEN: I wasn't nasty to him. Besides, I couldn't talk to you in front him, could I? Hey, wait till you see these things for the baby.

JO: You hurt people's feelings and you don't even notice.

HELEN: Jo, I just wanted to get rid of him, that's all. Look at those, Jo. Look, isn't that pretty, eh? The baby's going to be dressed like a prince, isn't he?

JO: We're all princes in our own little kingdom. You're not to insult Geoffrey. Will you leave him alone?

HELEN: Hey, look at this Jo, isn't it pretty? Oh, I love babies— aren't they lovely?

JO: Has your husband thrown you out?

HELEN: Oh come off it, Jo. I had to be with you at a time like this, hadn't I? And what about this sailor lad of yours, have you made any attempt to trace him? He's entitled to keep his child, you know.

JO: I wouldn't do that, it's degrading.

HELEN: What do you call this set-up?

JO: It's all right. There's no need for you to worry about me. I can work for the baby myself.

HELEN: Who's going to look after it when you're out at work? Have you thought about that?

JO: Yes, I have.

HELEN: Well, you can't do two jobs at once, you know. Who's going to nurse it? Him?

JO: That's my business, I can do anything when I set my mind to it.

HELEN: Very clever, aren't you?

JO: There's no need to be so superior. Look where all your swanking's landed you. What does the little lady want—an engagement ring? And now he's thrown you out, hasn't he, and you have to come crawling back here.

HELEN: Well, it was good while it lasted.

JO: Making a fool of yourself over that throw-back.

HELEN: He threw his money about like a man with no arms.

JO: This is my flat now, Helen.

HELEN: It's all right, love, I've got a bit of money put by.

JO: You're a real fool, aren't you?

HELEN: Oh, Jo, look. I'm back aren't I? Forget it. Don't keep on about it.

JO: Do you know what I think?

HELEN: What?

JO: I think you're still in love with him.

HELEN: In love? Me?

JO: Yes.

HELEN: You must be mad.

JO: What happened?

HELEN: He's gone off with his bit of crumpet. Still, it was good while it lasted. Anyway. I'll shift some of this, Jo.

JO: So we're back where we started. And all those months you stayed away from me because of him! Just like when I was small.

HELEN: I never thought about you! It's a funny thing, I never have done when I've been happy. But these last few weeks I've known I should be with you.

JO: So you stayed away—

HELEN: Yes. I can't stand trouble.

JO: Oh, there's no trouble. I've been performing a perfectly normal, healthy function. We're wonderful! Do you know, for the first time in my life I feel really important. I feel as though I could take care of the whole world. I even feel as though I could take care of you, too!

HELEN: Here, I forgot to tell you, I've ordered a lovely cot for you.

JO: We've got one.

HELEN: It's lovely. It's got pink curtains, you know, and frills. [JO *gets wicker basket from under bed.*]
Oh, I don't like that. What is it?

JO: It's wicker work. Geof got it.

HELEN: It's a bit old-fashioned, isn't it?

JO: We like it.

HELEN: Look love, why don't you go and lie down? You look as though you've got a bit of a headache.

JO: Do you wonder?

HELEN: Well, go and have a rest, there's a good girl. I'm going to tidy this place up for you. I'm going to make it just the way you like it. Go on.

JO: Oh no!

HELEN: Go on, Jo. Go on. It looks more like a laundry basket, doesn't it! Oh! The state of this place! We'll never have it right. Living like pigs in a pigsty—

[GEOFFREY *enters.*]

Oh, you're back are you? Well, come in if you're coming.

GEOF: Where's Jo?

HELEN: She's in bed. Where do you think she is? She's having a little sleep, so don't you dare wake her up.

GEOF: I wouldn't do that. [*He places pack filled with food on the table.*]

HELEN: Don't put that bag on there, I'm cleaning this place up.

GEOF: You know I just did it before you came.

HELEN: It doesn't look like it. Look, son, we're going to have the midwife running in and out of here before long. We want this place all clean and tidy, all hygienic-looking, if that's possible.

GEOF: Well, it's clean.

JO: Is that Geof?

HELEN: Now look what you've done!

GEOF: Yes, Jo.

JO: Have you got any of those headache pills, love?

GEOF: Yes, I'll get you some.

HELEN: If you're going in there take these flowers with you and put them in water. You might as well make yourself useful. They look as though they're withering away. [*She peers into the pack.*] What the devil's he got here? What's that? Spaghetti! I don't know how people can eat it. And that's a funny looking lettuce. What the hell's that? Hey, what's this here?

GEOF: What?

HELEN: All this muck in here?

GEOF: Well, Jo likes that type of food.

HELEN: Since when? She needs proper food down her at a time like this.

GEOF: Oh!

[HELEN *points to wicker basket.*]

HELEN: Hey, you can throw that bloody thing out for a start.

GEOF: What thing?

HELEN: That thing there. You're not putting my grandchild in a thing like that. Oh, this place! It's filthy! I don't know what you've been doing between the two of you. You might have kept it a bit cleaner than this. Just look at it! Don't stand there looking silly holding that thing, throw it away, or do something with it! I've ordered a proper cot of the latest design, it's got all the etceteras and everything. This place! You're living like pigs in a pigsty. Oh, for God's sake give it here, I'll do something with it.

GEOF: Yes, but Jo likes it.

HELEN: Well, I suppose it will come in handy for something [*She enters the kitchen.*] Oh my God, it's the same in here! Nowhere to put anything . . . Are you off now?

GEOF: Yes.

HELEN: Well, take that muck with you as you're going.

GEOF: I don't want it.

HELEN: I'm sure I don't.

GEOF: Mrs. Smith, I . . . I . . .

HELEN: Are you talking to me?

GEOF: Yes, I wanted to ask you something.

HELEN: Well, get it said. Don't mumble.

GEOF: I don't want you to take offence.

HELEN: Do I look the type that takes offence?

GEOF: Would you not frighten Jo?

HELEN: I thought you said you were going.

GEOF: I said would you not frighten Jo.

HELEN: What are you talking about, frightening her?

GEOF: You know, telling her that it might be tricky or that she might have trouble, because she's going to be all right.

HELEN: Are you trying to tell me what to do with my own daughter?

GEOF: Oh no.

HELEN: Well, are you going?

GEOF: Yes, although she said she didn't want a woman with
her when she had it.

HELEN: She said what?

GEOF: She said she wanted me with her when she had it
because she said she wouldn't be frightened if I was with
her.

HELEN: How disgusting!

GEOF: There's nothing disgusting about it.

HELEN: A man in the room at a time like this!

GEOF: Husbands stay with their wives.

HELEN: Are you her husband?

GEOF: No.

HELEN: Well, get.

GEOF: I'm going. She can't cope with the two of us. Only just
don't frighten her, that's all.

HELEN: I've told you we don't want that.

GEOF: Yes I know, but she likes it.

HELEN: You can bloody well take it with you, we don't want it.

[GEOFFREY *empties food from his pack on to the table while*
HELEN *thrusts it back.* HELEN *finally throws the whole thing,
pack and all, on to the floor.*]

GEOF: Yes, the one thing civilisation couldn't do anything
about—women. Good-bye Jo, and good luck. [*He goes.*]

[JO *stirs on the bed.*]

HELEN: It's all right, love, I'm here and everything's all right.
Are you awake now?

JO: Hello. Yes ... What's it like?

HELEN: What?

JO: Is there much pain?

HELEN: No! It's not so much pain as hard work, love. I was
putting my Christmas pudding up on a shelf when you
started on me. There I was standing on a chair singing
away merry as the day is long ...

JO: Did you yell?

HELEN: No, I ran.

JO: Do you know, I had such a funny dream just now.

HELEN: Oh Jo, you're always dreaming, aren't you. Well, don't let's talk about your dreams or we'll get morbid.

JO: Where would you like those flowers putting?

HELEN: Over ... over there ... Come on, you come and do it, love.

JO: Hasn't Geof come back yet?

HELEN: No, he hasn't.

JO: Well, where are you going to sleep, Helen?

HELEN: It's all right, love. Don't fall over, now.

JO: You know, I've got so used to old Geof lying there on that couch like—like an old watchdog. You aren't ...

HELEN: It's all right, love, don't you worry about me, I'll find somewhere.

JO: I wonder where he is ... Oh!

HELEN: Oh Jo, careful ... Hold on, love, hold on! It'll be all right. The first one doesn't last long. Oh my God, I could do with a drink now. Hold on.

[JO *kneels on bed,* HELEN *strokes her hair.*]

JO: That's better.

HELEN: Are you all right now? There we are. [*Children sing outside.*] Can you hear those children singing over there on the croft, Jo?

JO: Yes, you can always hear them on still days.

HELEN: You know when I was young we used to play all day long at this time of the year; in the summer we had singing games and in the spring we played with tops and hoops, and then in the autumn there was the Fifth of November, then we used to have bonfires in the street, and gingerbread and all that. Have I ever told you about the time when we went to a place called Shining Clough? Oh, I must have done. I used to climb up there every day and sit on the top of the hill, and you could see the mills in the distance, but the clough itself was covered in moss. Isn't it funny how you remember these things? Do you know, I'd sit there all day long and nobody ever knew where I was. Shall I go and make us a cup of tea?

[HELEN *enters kitchen and fiddles with stove.*]

Oh Jo, I've forgotten how we used to light this thing.

JO: Turn on all the knobs. Mind you don't gas yourself.

HELEN: I still can't do it.

JO: Geof'll fix it.

HELEN: No, it's all right.

JO: Helen.

HELEN: Yes.

JO: My baby may be black.

HELEN: You what, love?

JO: My baby will be black.

HELEN: Oh, don't be silly, Jo. You'll be giving yourself nightmares.

JO: But it's true. He was black.

HELEN: Who?

JO: Jimmie.

HELEN: You mean to say that ... that sailor was a black man? ... Oh my God! Nothing else can happen to me now. Can you see me wheeling a pram with a ... Oh my God. I'll have to have a drink.

JO: What are you going to do?

HELEN: I don't know. Drown it. Who knows about it?

JO: Geoffrey.

HELEN: And what about the nurse? She's going to get a bit of a shock, isn't she?

JO: Well, she's black too.

HELEN: Good, perhaps she'll adopt it. Dear God in heaven!

JO: If you don't like it you can get out. I didn't ask you to come here.

HELEN: Where's my hat?

JO: On your head.

HELEN: Oh yes ... I don't know what's to be done with you, I don't really. [*To the audience.*] I ask you, what would you do?

JO: Are you going?

HELEN: Yes.

JO: Are you just going for a drink?

HELEN: Yes.

JO: Are you coming back?

HELEN: Yes.

JO: Well, what are you going to do?

HELEN: Put it on the stage and call it Blackbird. [*She rushes out.*]

[JO *watches her go, leaning against the doorpost. Then she looks round the room, smiling a little to herself—she remembers* GEOF.]

JO: As I was going up Pippin Hill,
Pippin Hill was dirty.
And there I met a pretty miss,
And she dropped me a curtsy.
Little miss, pretty miss,
Blessings light upon you.
If I had half a crown a day,
I'd gladly spend it on you.

Curtain.

Notes

Act One

7   *Manchester*: a large industrial city in the north of England. According to a note under the cast list on p. 6, the play takes place in Salford, a smaller industrial town – where Delaney grew up – adjoining Manchester.

7   *living off her immoral earnings*: it is a criminal offence for a man to live off a woman's immoral earnings, i.e. her earnings as a prostitute. Jo is having a joke at her mother's expense, making out that her mother is more sexually promiscuous than she actually is. While Delaney describes Helen as a 'semi-whore' it is important to remember that Helen is not a professional sex worker.

7   *gasworks*: factory plant for the production of gas, typically an ugly, large, industrial building, hence the irony of Helen's comment about this being 'a lovely view'. Shot on location in Manchester, the film version captures this urban scene, juxtaposing, for example, an interior shot of Jo in the room with a skyline of smoking factory furnaces.

7   *contemporary*: in the decorative style of the fifties.

8   *one of those shilling in the slot affairs*: a meter for the gas that needs money. A shilling was a silver coin (pre-decimalisation in 1971), the equivalent of five new pence.

10   *Perhaps he's one of the fixtures*: meaning perhaps he comes with the room. Helen is getting her own back by teasing Jo about not having had a boyfriend.

12   *knocked me into the middle of next week*: hit me very hard.

12   *aspirins*: painkilling tablets.

13   *vamp it*: add a simple improvisation or accompaniment.

14   *geniused*: Jo has made this word up. In the verbal dual with her mother she's laying claim to natural brilliance.

15   *all this flitting about*: flitting is a colloquial term for moving home. Jo is expressing her exasperation about the way in which Helen is constantly making them move from place to place.

15   *communal latrine and wash-house*: meaning shared toilet and bathroom. This is a further indication of how poor Jo and

Helen are. However it was usual at the time for cheap lodging
houses to have communal bathrooms and toilets.

16 *Look what the wind's blown in*: meaning, 'Well, look who's
here', an expression often reserved for unexpected visitors.

16 *new headquarters*: a militaristic turn of phrase reflecting Peter's
army background. As a rather grand term to describe the
room, it suggests a note of comic mockery.

17 *I was throwing my hand in*: meaning Helen was giving up on
the relationship with Peter.

18 *the old firm*: colloquial term for a reliable, familiar enterprise.
Peter is referring to their relationship as familiar, established,
trying to encourage Helen not to give up on it.

18 *girdle*: old-fashioned, corset-type of women's underwear,
usually elasticated.

18 *'Walter, Walter, lead me to the altar!'*: a line from a song of
that title.

19 *'I see a quiet place, a fireplace, a cosy room'*: a line from the
song 'My Blue Heaven'.

20 *A rich, dark, Havana . . .*: the sort of description found in
advertising slogans.

22 *institution*: institution or hospital for the insane – Jo's way of
saying her mother must be mad for wanting to get married
again.

22 *coloured*: acceptable term of reference (at that time) for people
of ethnic minority origins.

22 *naval rating*: ordinary sailor.

23 *I don't know why I love you but I do*: title line of a popular
song.

23 *she isn't prejudiced against colour*: Jo is trying to reassure Boy
that Helen will not be racially prejudiced against him. Behind
this comment is a hint of 1950s Britain in which racist attitudes
escalated as the first wave of black immigration took place
(generally associated with the arrival of the *Empire Windrush*
ship in 1948, carrying the first generation of immigrants from
the Caribbean). See also Jo and Boy's discussion of his racial
origins on p. 25, and Helen's reaction when she finds out Jo's
baby is black, p. 86.

25 *Mau-Mau*: nationalist movement based on the Kikuyu tribe in
Kenya in the 1950s during the struggle for independence.

27 *national service*: compulsory two years in the armed forces to
which all young men were conscripted at this time.

27 *I was a Teenage*: several films, usually horror films, had titles

beginning like this, e.g. *I was a Teenage Frankenstein* (released in 1957). Helen leaves the title incomplete for comic effect.

27 *The Ten Commandments*: an epic film by Cecil B. De Mille based on the Bible (released in 1958).

27 *Desire Under the . . .*: the film version of Eugene O'Neill's intense drama, *Desire Under the Elms* was released in 1958. Again Helen gets fun out of leaving the title incomplete and introducing a note of comic sexual innuendo.

28 *I'd sooner be put on't streets*: Jo is saying she would rather be a sex worker (than have a film career).

29 *spiv*: flashily dressed person living on his wits.

29 *Arabian Knight*: *The Arabian Nights* is a series of ancient oriental tales, purportedly told by Scheherazade, the bride of a sultan, to stave off her execution. Helen is making a pun.

30 *glad rags*: best or party clothes.

33 *'That wild, destructive thing called love'*: a line from a popular song.

34 *Lord's Day Observance Society*: a group who believe that Sunday, the Christian Sabbath, should be kept holy. Peter means that Jo is being unusually moral and righteous.

34 *Blackpool*: a seaside resort in the north-west of England, famous for its Tower, within easy reach of Manchester and Salford, and noted for its working-class culture and popular entertainment (variety shows, amusement arcades, etc.). The film version includes a Blackpool outing, featuring the Tower, the seafront fair, and the side shows.

35 *called to the bar*: usually said of barristers when they first enter their profession. Helen is making fun of Jo's new job in a bar/pub, and Jo turns the joke back on Peter given that the pub is one of his favourite haunts.

35 *black hole of Calcutta*: popular saying, meaning a dark, confined space; originally the dungeon in which the sultan who captured Calcutta in 1756 crowded his enemies.

36 *opium pellet*: Jo is teasing Boy about the idea that he might drug and take advantage of her sexually.

36 *Pirate King*: Boy is referring to Peter. Pirate kings in children's stories are often portrayed with a black eye-patch like Peter's.

37 *You've had your chips*: too late, you've missed your chance.

38 *Woolworths*: chain store associated with the sale of cheap rather than quality goods.

38 *Do you object to the 'gross clasps of the lascivious Moor'?, etc.*: Boy starts quoting from Shakespeare's *Othello*, using this as a point of cultural reference for the mixed-race romance between himself and Jo.

40 *spends his money like water*: he spends his money recklessly (although not, as it turns out, on Helen, see p. 80).

42 *down-and-out boozer knocking back the meths*: Jo is suggesting her mother will turn into an alcoholic tramp, drinking methylated spirits, a cheap but toxic form of alcohol to which homeless and penniless drinkers sometimes resort out of desperation.

42 *Old Nick*: the devil.

44 *half-wit*: this image that Helen creates of Jo's father is one that comes to haunt and concern Jo throughout her pregnancy (see note for p. 73 on Ibsen's *Ghosts*.)

44 *Puritan*: originally a member of an extreme English Protestant party, strict in religion and morals; used of someone who disapproves of sex.

Act Two

47 *maisonette*: normally a flat on two floors.

47 *up the creek*: slang meaning all wrong, mistaken. The full saying is 'up the creek without a paddle' and Geof is using it here to refer to the fact that he can't find his way around the flat in the dark.

47 *under the arches*: a reference to sleeping rough – arches under bridges give some shelter to the homeless out on the streets.

48 *people like you*: meaning men who are gay, which is how Jo reads Geof's sexuality.

51 *Spratts*: a well-known make of dog biscuit.

51 *Jack Spratt . . . clean*: a nursery rhyme.

54 *walking away*: i.e. with head lice.

54 *bit deficient*: again suggests Jo's preoccupation with the idea of inherited abnormality.

57 *croft*: (dialect) patch of waste land.

57 *if I started something*: meaning if Geof started a physical, sexual relationship with Jo. Given Geof's sexuality and Jo, who feels disappointed and let down after her relationship with Boy, this is not going to work, as the aborted kissing sequence on p. 58 illustrates.

59 *Romeo*: male lover, from Shakespeare's *Romeo and Juliet*. This is Helen having one of her many digs at Geof's sexuality.

60 *What blew you in?*: meaning, 'What's brought you here?' The question comes with a sense of foreboding, of an 'ill wind' that's blown Helen back into Jo's life. (See also note to p. 16).

61   *organ grinder . . . monkey, etc.*: Helen wants to talk to the person in charge. This comes from a popular expression (a reference to street musicians performing with pet monkeys) and Helen is rudely implying that the relationship between Geof and Jo is like that between an organ grinder and his monkey.

61   *Christmas box*: present traditionally given to tradesmen, etc., at Christmas. Here used sarcastically.

61   *When the cat's away*: a proverb, meaning that people get up to all sorts of things they shouldn't when nobody's around to check on them. The full saying is: When the cat's away, the mice do play.

61   *Sling your hook*: slang, go away.

61   *Can you cut the bread on it yet?*: at an advanced stage of pregnancy the belly sticks out high and shelf-like. Helen is trying to confirm how far along Jo is in her pregnancy.

63   *pansified little freak*: 'pansy' is a term of homophobic abuse, which Helen is giving vent to in her anger over Jo's pregnancy and the unconventional living arrangement she has with Geof. The homophobic abuse of Geof by Helen (and by Peter) reflects the prevailing attitude at that time towards gay men, who were often ostracised, stigmatised and ridiculed on account of their sexuality. Despite the Wolfenden committee and its Report in 1957, which advocated a more liberal view of homosexuality through its recommendation that homosexual relations conducted in private between consenting adults should no longer be considered a criminal offence, it was ten years before the Sexual Offences Act in 1967 legislated for a partial decriminalisation of homosexual acts.

64   *maternity benefit*: weekly payments made to expectant mothers by the government.

65   *Temperance Society*: a society abstaining from alcohol. Calling Peter the president, Helen is being highly sarcastic.

65   *bun in the oven*: slang for pregnant.

65   *'Getting to know you'*: title line of a song from the musical *The King and I*, the film version of which had been released in 1956.

65   *unrestored oil painting*: meaning that Helen is showing her age, is no longer a great beauty.

65   *bubble belly*: offensive reference to Jo's pregnancy.

65   *Oedipus*: Peter is referring to himself here, comparing his relationship with Helen (as a woman older than himself) to that of Oedipus who unwittingly married his own mother, Jocasta.

66 *picked up a couple of grapefruit*: meaning Peter has picked up and gone off with a younger woman. His sexist discourse is degrading to women generally and to Helen specifically, all of which gives the audience further insight into how badly wrong the relationship between them has gone.

66 *smallest room*: toilet.

67 *leapfrog*: a children's game in which they jump over the backs of several others.

68 *little fruitcake parcel*: expression of homophobic abuse.

68 *not having this shower at any price*: Peter refuses to have anything to do with Jo, Geof, and even Helen if she chooses them over him.

69 *flying flip*: flying jump.

69 *here endeth*: said after a reading from the Bible in the Church of England service.

70 *Little Women*: a nineteenth-century novel for girls by Louisa May Alcott; its tone is very moral.

70 *Edwardian ... Ted*: Edward VII reigned from 1901 to 1910, a period known as Edwardian. But in the 1950s it was fashionable for young men, mainly from the working class, to dress in a style slightly like that of the Edwardian period, from which came the label 'Teddy boys' or 'Teds'.

72 *'And he took up his bed and walked'*: a reference to the New Testament miracle where Jesus cures a sick man.

73 *Irish*: often used of something comically contradictory.

73 *Ibsen's Ghosts*: Ibsen's play in which the sexual sins of an absent father are visited on the son, who, it is revealed, has congenital syphilis. In his own way Geof is trying to reassure Jo, making out that Helen has exaggerated or sensationalised the family 'drama' about Jo's father, trying to disabuse her of the idea that there might be something wrong either with herself or the baby because of a (mental) illness inherited from her father.

73 *put away for treatment*: Geof means that Helen looks at him as someone who should be institutionalised on account of his sanity, or possibly his sexuality. In the 1950s, aversion therapy treatment was used to 'cure' homosexuality as a deviant sexuality.

74 *patrol leader in the Boy Scouts*: the Boy Scouts is a world-wide

organisation for boys; patrol leader is a boy who leads a small group within a company.

74 *Scoutmaster*: sensational newspapers sometimes feature stories about Scoutmasters abusing their position as leaders of a Scout company, making sexually inappropriate advances to the boys. It has become a journalistic cliché.

74 *a few holds*: grips used in wrestling.

75 *digs*: lodgings.

77 *Flying Doctor*: a television series based on the adventures of Australian doctors who flew to emergency cases by aeroplane.

80 *entitled to keep his child*: Helen might mean that the father has a legal obligation to pay for the upbringing of his child, or she might simply mean that Jo should pass the child over to him.

80 *threw his money about like a man with no arms*: was very mean with money.

83 *etceteras*: extra equipment and trimmings.

85 *Clough*: a dialect word (pronounced: cluff) meaning gorge or narrow ravine.

Questions for further study

1. Discuss the significance of the title of the play in relation to the themes and characters.
2. 'When I met your father I was as pure and unsullied as I fondly, and perhaps mistakenly, image you to be' (Helen, p. 44). In what ways is Jo both like and unlike her mother? How might the similarities and differences between them be developed in rehearsal?
3. The original production of the play was described as being 'a sort of magnified realism in which everything is like life but somehow larger than life'. How would you describe the genre of the play and go about finding an appropriate performance style for it?
4. To what extent do the comical elements in *A Taste of Honey* make it difficult for an audience to take the characters and their situation seriously?
5. 'The women in the play are the only well-rounded characters.' To what extent do you agree with this statement?
6. *A Taste of Honey* has remained popular ever since its first performance. What is it about the play that maintains its appeal? How good a play do you think it is and why?
7. The play is set in Salford in the late 1950s. How important is it to retain the location and the period of the play? What would you do to bring this out in performance or what justification would you make for changing the play's setting and/or period?
8. 'The world is littered with women I've rejected, women still anxious to indulge my little vices and excuse my less seemly virtues' (Peter, p. 19). How do you account for the attraction between Helen and Peter?
9. Jo and Helen seemed locked in a world of their own making. What is it about their relationship that an audience finds so appealing?
10. In order to provide smoother transitions between the scenes, Joan Littlewood used a live jazz band and had the characters dancing out of one scene and into the next. How effective is this as a dramatic device? What other methods might you use to move

from one scene to another and why?

11. There has been much debate about the impact that Joan Littlewood's working methods as a director had on the final version of the script. There are moments in the play when characters speak to the audience or dance on and off to music. What is the significance of the non-realistic elements of the play and what do they tell you about Joan Littlewood's directorial style?

12. 'My usual self is a very unusual self, Geoffrey Ingram, and don't you forget it. I'm an extraordinary person. There's only one of me like there's only one of you' (Jo, p. 50). What are the unique qualities about Jo and how would you develop these through the rehearsal process?

13. The circumstances that Jo finds herself in could be considered tragic but Shelagh Delaney chooses to use comedy to lighten the mood of the play. How is the comedy created in the text and how would you bring this out in performance?

14. Jo and Helen seem content to accept their circumstances almost without question. How does a play in which the leading characters lack ambition or seem indifferent to improving their situation sustain an audience's interest?

15. *A Taste of Honey* is the work of a nineteen-year-old playwright. Some critics consider the immaturity of the writing to be the play's weakness while others consider the freshness of the writing to be its strength. Where do you stand in this argument and why?

16. Helen's line on p. 11, 'What a damn silly place to put a window', was apparently an ad lib by Avis Bunnage, the actress who created the role, when she noticed the stage crew installing part of the set during the technical rehearsal. How would you create a suitable setting, using limited resources like the original production?

17. In the original ending of the play, Jo was whisked off to hospital to have her baby and Geof was left lying on the couch with a baby doll to commit suicide. How does this compare with the published ending and why do you think it was changed?

18. 'This is not so much dramaturgy as anthropology.' To what extent do you consider *A Taste of Honey* to be a study of working-class life in 1950s northern England?

19. Joan Littlewood felt that the most difficult character to make believable in the play was Geof. To what extent do you think she succeeded in making Geof believable?

20. The only unnamed character is 'Boy'. Why is this and how does this character function in the play?

Methuen Drama Student Editions

Jean Anouilh *Antigone* • John Arden *Serjeant Musgrave's Dance*
Alan Ayckbourn *Confusions* • Aphra Behn *The Rover*
Edward Bond *Lear* • Bertolt Brecht *The Caucasian Chalk Circle*
Life of Galileo • *Mother Courage and her Children*
The Resistible Rise of Arturo Ui • *The Threepenny Opera*
Anton Chekhov *The Cherry Orchard* • *The Seagull* • *Three Sisters*
Uncle Vanya • Caryl Churchill *Serious Money* • *Top Girls*
Shelagh Delaney *A Taste of Honey* • Euripides *Elektra* • *Medea*
Dario Fo *Accidental Death of an Anarchist* • Michael Frayn *Copenhagen*
John Galsworthy *Strife* • Nikolai Gogol *The Government Inspector*
Robert Holman *Across Oka* • Henrik Ibsen *A Doll's House* • *Ghosts*
Hedda Gabler • Charlotte Keatley *My Mother Said I Never Should*
Bernard Kops *Dreams of Anne Frank* • Federico García Lorca
Blood Wedding • *Doña Rosita the Spinster* (bilingual edition) • *The House
of Bernarda Alba* • (bilingual edition) • *Yerma* (bilingual edition) • David
Mamet *Glengarry Glen Ross* • *Oleanna* • Patrick Marber *Closer* • John
Marston *The Malcontent* • Joe Orton *Loot* • Luigi Pirandello *Six
Characters in Search of an Author* • Mark Ravenhill *Shopping and
F***ing* • Willy Russell *Blood Brothers* • *Educating Rita* • Sophocles
Antigone • *Oedipus the King* • Wole Soyinka *Death and the King's
Horseman* • August Strindberg *Miss Julie* • J. M. Synge *The Playboy
of the Western World* • Theatre Workshop *Oh What a Lovely War*
Timberlake Wertenbaker *Our Country's Good* • Arnold Wesker *The
Merchant* • Oscar Wilde *The Importance of Being Earnest* • Tennessee
Williams *A Streetcar Named Desire* • *The Glass Menagerie*

Methuen Drama Modern Plays

include work by

Edward Albee
Jean Anouilh
John Arden
Margaretta D'Arcy
Peter Barnes
Sebastian Barry
Brendan Behan
Dermot Bolger
Edward Bond
Bertolt Brecht
Howard Brenton
Anthony Burgess
Simon Burke
Jim Cartwright
Caryl Churchill
Complicite
Noël Coward
Lucinda Coxon
Sarah Daniels
Nick Darke
Nick Dear
Shelagh Delaney
David Edgar
David Eldridge
Dario Fo
Michael Frayn
John Godber
Paul Godfrey
David Greig
John Guare
Peter Handke
David Harrower
Jonathan Harvey
Iain Heggie
Declan Hughes
Terry Johnson
Sarah Kane
Charlotte Keatley
Barrie Keeffe

Howard Korder
Robert Lepage
Doug Lucie
Martin McDonagh
John McGrath
Terrence McNally
David Mamet
Patrick Marber
Arthur Miller
Mtwa, Ngema & Simon
Tom Murphy
Phyllis Nagy
Peter Nichols
Sean O'Brien
Joseph O'Connor
Joe Orton
Louise Page
Joe Penhall
Luigi Pirandello
Stephen Poliakoff
Franca Rame
Mark Ravenhill
Philip Ridley
Reginald Rose
Willy Russell
Jean-Paul Sartre
Sam Shepard
Wole Soyinka
Simon Stephens
Shelagh Stephenson
Peter Straughan
C. P. Taylor
Theatre Workshop
Sue Townsend
Judy Upton
Timberlake Wertenbaker
Roy Williams
Snoo Wilson
Victoria Wood

Methuen Drama Contemporary Dramatists

include

John Arden (two volumes)
Arden & D'Arcy
Peter Barnes (three volumes)
Sebastian Barry
Dermot Bolger
Edward Bond (eight volumes)
Howard Brenton
  (two volumes)
Richard Cameron
Jim Cartwright
Caryl Churchill (two volumes)
Sarah Daniels (two volumes)
Nick Darke
David Edgar (three volumes)
David Eldridge
Ben Elton
Dario Fo (two volumes)
Michael Frayn (three volumes)
John Godber (three volumes)
Paul Godfrey
David Greig
John Guare
Lee Hall (two volumes)
Peter Handke
Jonathan Harvey
  (two volumes)
Declan Hughes
Terry Johnson (three volumes)
Sarah Kane
Barrie Keefe
Bernard-Marie Koltès
  (two volumes)
Franz Xaver Kroetz
David Lan
Bryony Lavery
Deborah Levy
Doug Lucie

David Mamet (four volumes)
Martin McDonagh
Duncan McLean
Anthony Minghella
  (two volumes)
Tom Murphy (five volumes)
Phyllis Nagy
Anthony Neilson
Philip Osment
Gary Owen
Louise Page
Stewart Parker (two volumes)
Joe Penhall
Stephen Poliakoff
  (three volumes)
David Rabe
Mark Ravenhill
Christina Reid
Philip Ridley
Willy Russell
Eric-Emmanuel Schmitt
Ntozake Shange
Sam Shepard (two volumes)
Wole Soyinka (two volumes)
Simon Stephens
Shelagh Stephenson
David Storey (three volumes)
Sue Townsend
Judy Upton
Michel Vinaver
  (two volumes)
Arnold Wesker (two volumes)
Michael Wilcox
Roy Williams (two volumes)
Snoo Wilson (two volumes)
David Wood (two volumes)
Victoria Wood

Methuen Drama Classical Greek Dramatists

Aeschylus Plays: One
(Persians, Seven Against Thebes, Suppliants,
Prometheus Bound)

Aeschylus Plays: Two
(Oresteia: Agamemnon, Libation-Bearers, Eumenides)

Aristophanes Plays: One
(Acharnians, Knights, Peace, Lysistrata)

Aristophanes Plays: Two
(Wasps, Clouds, Birds, Festival Time, Frogs)

Aristophanes & Menander: New Comedy
(Women in Power, Wealth, The Malcontent,
The Woman from Samos)

Euripides Plays: One
(Medea, The Phoenician Women, Bacchae)

Euripides Plays: Two
(Hecuba, The Women of Troy, Iphigeneia at Aulis,
Cyclops)

Euripides Plays: Three
(Alkestis, Helen, Ion)

Euripides Plays: Four
(Elektra, Orestes, Iphigeneia in Tauris)

Euripides Plays: Five
(Andromache, Herakles' Children, Herakles)

Euripides Plays: Six
(Hippolytos, Suppliants, Rhesos)

Sophocles Plays: One
(Oedipus the King, Oedipus at Colonus, Antigone)

Sophocles Plays: Two
(Ajax, Women of Trachis, Electra, Philoctetes)

Methuen Drama World Classics

include

Jean Anouilh (two volumes)
Brendan Behan
Aphra Behn
Bertolt Brecht (eight volumes)
Büchner
Bulgakov
Calderón
Čapek
Anton Chekhov
Noël Coward (eight volumes)
Feydeau
Eduardo De Filippo
Max Frisch
John Galsworthy
Gogol
Gorky (two volumes)
Harley Granville Barker
  (two volumes)
Victor Hugo
Henrik Ibsen (six volumes)
Jarry

Lorca (three volumes)
Marivaux
Mustapha Matura
David Mercer (two volumes)
Arthur Miller (five volumes)
Molière
Musset
Peter Nichols (two volumes)
Joe Orton
A. W. Pinero
Luigi Pirandello
Terence Rattigan
  (two volumes)
W. Somerset Maugham
  (two volumes)
August Strindberg
  (three volumes)
J. M. Synge
Ramón del Valle-Inclán
Frank Wedekind
Oscar Wilde